BOOK TWO

CHANGED LIVES

Ten True Stories: *From Addiction to Freedom*

compiled by
PASCO A. MANZO

FOREWORD BY MATTHEW WEST

Changed Lives (Book Two)
Ten True Stories: From Addiction to Freedom
Compiled by Pasco A. Manzo

Teen Challenge New England, Inc.
1315 Main Street
Brockton, MA 02301

Edited by Josiah D. Manzo and Karen Henriksen
Cover / Layout Design by Justin Palojarvi
Photos by Colton Simmons and Rachel Manzo

ISBN: 978-0-692-52628-6

Printed in the United States of America
2015 - First Edition

Dedication

I dedicate this book…
to all those who have struggled
and have overcome the power of addiction.
You are today's heroes who bring hope
for tomorrow's overcomers.

"To him who overcomes
I will grant to sit with me on my throne,
as I also overcame and sat down
with my Father on His throne."

Revelation 3:21

Contents

Back Page Contents

Foreword

Matthew West

As a preacher's kid growing up in the suburbs of Chicago, Illinois, my Sunday mornings were spent in the front row of my father's church seated next to my two brothers and my mother. Most Sundays, my father would deliver the message but occasionally, a special guest speaker would visit our church. I'll never forget the first time that special guest was the group from Chicago's Teen Challenge. Sunday mornings had a tendency to feel routine for a preacher's kid. But there was something different about this group. My attention span was short and my thoughts were prone to wander to that baseball game that would follow Sunday service or where we might go out to eat for lunch. But this particular Sunday, I was on the edge of my seat as I witnessed some of the most authentic, vulnerable, and genuine glimpses of God's redeeming work displayed through the lives of the men who stood on that platform. Together they formed a choir, and sang their hearts out in worship. Now, it was clear most of these guys had no prior vocal training, many of them couldn't even carry a tune! However, that didn't stop them from making a joyful noise, and I could tell that they felt every single word they were singing, about a God who changes lives and restores hope.

Looking back, I have a greater understanding why those Teen Challenge Sundays had such a profound impact on me. What I was witnessing on those Sundays was something authentic, something real. These people weren't putting on a smile and pretending that they were living the perfect life. Instead, they were stepping up on stage and publicly proclaiming that they were far from perfect, but that their lives had been changed by a perfect God. It was that kind of genuine expression of faith that awakened something inside me, and still calls to me today. I want that kind of authenticity, and God desires that kind of authenticity for me and for you. Too often we get too caught up in what other people think of us. So, we try to control what they think by making sure we present ourselves in just the right light, like we've got it all together. But now more than ever, that's not what a lost and hurting world needs to see. Just like that little kid in the front row of his father's church, the world will be awakened by the stories of real life change brought about by the touch of the healing hands of Jesus.

This book is filled with one powerful story after another of God's redeeming work in everyday people like you and me.

These stories remind us that we all have hurts, habits, and hang ups and that we are all broken. Teen Challenge is an incredible ministry. But Teen Challenge alone can't change a life. Teen challenge knows that God is in the business of restoration, and these stories will show you how He can flood even the most desperate and hurting heart with hope and turn a life in a new direction.

Introduction
Addiction

Pasco A. Manzo

Ad-dic-tion: the origin of the word stems back from 1595-1605; Latin *addiction* (stem of addictiō) a giving over, surrender. The root word is "addict", in Greek its *"diké"*, justice, rights. Something like *"adiktoi"* could mean, "those not entitled to rights", therefore slaves.

The following are a few dictionary definitions for the word addiction; *Merriam-Webster Dictionary:* compulsive need for and use of a habit-forming substance (as heroin, nicotine, or alcohol) characterized by tolerance and by well-defined physiological symptoms upon withdrawal. *Broadly:* persistent compulsive use of a substance known by the user to be harmful. *Dictionary.com:* the state of being enslaved to a habit or practice or to something that is psychologically or physically habit forming, as narcotics, to such an extent that its cessation causes severe trauma. *British Dictionary:*

the condition of being abnormally dependent on some habit, especially compulsive dependency on narcotic drugs. In summary, it's someone who is a slave with no rights and has abnormal behavior with compulsive dependency. It is quite a grim picture.

When I think of the word addiction many other words also come to mind: hopeless, bound, trapped, hurt, depressed, dependent, confused, controlled, stuck, entombed, reliant, helpless, vulnerable, powerless, burdened, weighted, destitute, problem, captivity, oppression, repression, domination, bondage, and desperation. I am sure you could add to that list, especially if you or a loved one is personally familiar with an addiction.

People get addicted to many things such as illegal drugs, prescription drugs, alcohol, nicotine, pornography, food, and gambling, to name a few. These are all harmful and steal the quality of life in one way or another.

More than 22 million Americans age 12 and older - nearly 9% of the U.S. population - use illegal drugs, according to the government's *2010 National Survey on Drug Use and Health.* The National Institutes of Health estimate that 2.1 million Americans are hooked on prescribed opioids and are in danger of turning to the black market for a stronger fix.

There are several myths associated with drug addiction but let me give you three common ones.

Myth #1: Drug Addiction Is The Individual's Choice

Most people believe that every addict has the choice to say yes or no, the choice to use drugs or not to and their addiction exists because the addict allows it to. This is not true. When drugs are consumed by an addict, the brain is "high jacked" affecting the addict's ability to control the level of their drug use. Addiction should be thought of as a brain disease which causes the addict to think they must comply with its demands. For the addict, there is no other option, the brain insists you must do drugs to survive. Most addiction creates an environment susceptible to stealing, lying, neglecting family and places the addict in whatever risky situation, it takes to satisfy the addiction. Psalm 103:3 says "He forgives all our sins and heals all of our disease."

Myth #2: Only Individuals With No Willpower Are Addicted To Drugs

Some people think it is only weak-minded individuals who develop an addiction. However, once again the brain plays a major role. In fact the levels of dopamine in the brain that have been altered from substance abuse generally take 12-18 months to readjust. One reason that Teen Challenge New England & New Jersey has such a high recovery rate is because the length of our program is 15 months with an optional six months apprenticeship.

The Mayo Clinic staff states people of any age, sex or economic status can become addicted to a drug. However, certain factors can affect the likelihood and speed of developing an addiction.

• **Family history of addiction.** Drug addiction is more common in some families and likely involves genetic predisposition. If you have a blood relative, such as a parent or sibling, with an addiction, you're at greater risk of developing one.

• **Being male.** Men are more likely to have problems with drugs than women are. However, progression of addictive disorders is known to be faster in females.

• **Having another mental health disorder.** If you have a mental health disorder such as depression, high anxiety, attention-deficit/hyperactivity disorder or post-traumatic stress disorder, you're more likely to become dependent on drugs.

• **Peer pressure.** Peer pressure is a strong factor in starting to use and abuse drugs, particularly for young people who are more susceptible to it.

• **Lack of family involvement.** Difficult family situations or lack of a bond with your parents or siblings may increase the risk of addiction, as can a lack of parental supervision.

Myth #3: Drug Addiction Is A Hopeless Condition

Once an alcoholic or drug addict, always one. Not true. The scripture says in Proverbs 13:12 "Hope deferred makes the heart sick, but a longing fulfilled is a tree of life." Some say that addiction will always need treatment and that you have to live with it the rest of your life, but it is also true that HELP and HOPE are available for every addict. Teen Challenge New England & New Jersey have seen countless people remain clean for multiple years, breaking the power of addiction and never going back to abusing substance. In the first *Changed Lives* book, its stories reflect this truth. The ten true stories in this second book are also proof of what the Teen Challenge program with Jesus Christ can do for anyone who desires a new life.

Substance abuse refers to the harmful use of psychoactive substances, including alcohol and illicit drugs.

Psychoactive substance use can lead to dependence syndrome, a cluster of behavioral, cognitive, and physiological phenomena that develops after repeated substance use. It typically includes a strong desire to take the drug, difficulty controlling drug use, and persisting in drug use despite harmful consequences. Additionally, a higher priority is given to drug use than to other activities and obligations, tolerance of the drug increases, and sometimes there are withdrawal side effects.

The power of addiction is so strong its victims cannot say NO to the very thing that is robbing them of the life they want to live. Saul of Tarsus, also known as Paul the Apostle, said it this way, "The thing that I want to do, I don't do and the thing that I don't want to do, is the thing I find myself doing. Who shall deliver me from this terrible state that I am in?"

The power of addiction separates the individual from their parents, siblings, spouse and even their own children. Their friends become alienated as bridges are burned while they seek to satisfy their addiction. Their integrity, dignity, pride, self-respect, and self-esteem slowly shatter. Their dreams, career, and all aspects of normal daily life dwindle as their newfound addiction takes precedence.

Addiction is no stranger to the rich and famous. President Obama was addicted to nicotine. Rush Limbaugh got hooked on OxyContin. Glenn Beck is a recovering alcoholic, as is Elton John, Eric Clapton, Anthony Hopkins, Judy Collins, Mel Gibson, and many more. Tiger Woods is a recovering sex addict - it's likely that Warren Beatty and Wilt Chamberlain were also. William Bennett's gambling habit was all over the news. Oprah acknowledges she's a carbohydrate addict. For Julia Cameron it was alcohol and drugs, just as it

was for McKenzie Phillips and Carrie Fisher.

Drug and alcohol detoxes, treatment centers, drug-counseling, and even jail time help in the recovery process, but for most addicts they do not have a lasting effect. Perhaps because the lie that is often told and believed is relapse is part of the recovery process.

> Psychiatrist M. Scott Peck, a self-confessed nicotine addict and author of The Road Less Traveled, offered his perspective in a lecture, "Addiction: The Sacred Disease." Dr. Peck's thesis: At birth, humans become separated from God. Everyone is aware of this separation, but some people are more attuned to it than others. They report a feeling of emptiness, a longing, what many refer to as "a hole in their soul." They sense that something is missing, but don't know what it is. At some point in their lives (often quite young) these sensitive souls stumble across something that makes them feel better. For some it's alcohol, for others it's sugar, drugs, shopping, sex, work, gambling, or some other substance or activity that hits the spot. "Ahh," they sigh, "I've found what's been missing. This is the answer to my

problems." They have discovered a new best friend -- **their drug of choice.** Peck pointed out that the alcoholic is really thirsty for Spirit, but he settles for spirits. Alcohol is simply a form of cheap grace, as are all addictive substances. What we humans really long for is a connection to God... alignment with the Holy... re-union with the Divine. It is a deeply spiritual hunger -- a longing to go home again, back to Source. But we're confused about what we're really hungry for, so we go looking for love in all the wrong places. We reach for anything to take the edge off, to smooth out life's rough spots, to help us make it through the night.

While coping with addiction and trying to recover, the high risk of overdose is malevolently present.

In **Massachusetts** from November 2013 to February 2014, just four months, there were 185 heroin deaths. Governor Patrick declared public health emergency.

In **Rhode Island** there were 232 drug overdoses in 2013 with the same amount again in 2014. As of March 16, 2015 there were 51 deaths. The Rhode Island state Health Director Michael Fine and others say the increased availability

of Narcan, a medication that can reverse the effects of an opioid overdose, likely helped keep the death toll from climbing even higher.

In **Connecticut**, there were at least 189 deaths from heroin overdose in 2013 and at least 151 people died of opioid overdoses during the first six months of 2014, according to the latest available figures from the office of the chief medical examiner.

In **Vermont**, the state's per capita rate for people being treated for heroin and opiate addiction is the second highest in the country. In state courts, there were 220 convictions in 2013 involving heroin-related cases, up from 106 in 2012, according to the Vermont Center for Justice Research. Vermont Gov. Peter Shumlin devoted his entire State of the State message to the Legislature to the heroin problem and what to do about it. "In every corner of our state, heroin and opiate drug addiction threatens us," Shumlin told the lawmakers. "It requires all of us to take action before the quality of life that we cherish so much is compromised."

In **Maine**, the number of residents who died of drug overdoses in 2014 hit a record number, according to an analysis released from the Office of the Attorney General. The analysis, done by Marcella Sorg of the Margaret Chase Smith Policy Center at the University of Maine, along with the Office of Chief Medical Examiner, found that 208 people in Maine died of drug overdoses – an increase of 18 percent over the previous year, when 176 died of drug overdoses.

In **New Hampshire**, *The Telegraph* on February 13, 2015 reported that the state released new data that shows the total number of confirmed deaths from drug overdoses in 2014 rose to at least 300, with the heaviest toll shifting from middle-aged victims to young adults aged 21 to 30.

In **New Jersey**, drug overdoses are increasing according to *Drug Policy Alliance,* overdose is now its leading cause of accidental death.

What are the signs of an overdose? According to *Harm Reduction Coalition:*

- Awake, but unable to talk
- Body is very limp
- Face is very pale or clammy
- Fingernails and lips turn blue or purplish black
- For lighter skinned people, the skin tone turns bluish purple
- For darker skinned people, the skin tone turns grayish or ashen
- Breathing is very slow and shallow, erratic, or has stopped
- Pulse (heartbeat) is slow, erratic, or not there at all
- Choking sounds, or a snore-like gurgling noise

(sometimes called the "death rattle")

- Vomiting
- Loss of consciousness
- Unresponsive to outside stimulus

If you see any of these symptoms in a friend or family member that may have been using drugs, call 911 and get help immediately.

Unfortunately, for many it is too late and death is inescapable. Far too many deaths for us not to get upset and far too many for us to stand by and do nothing. One hundred Americans die of a drug overdose every day (*The Washington Post* February 7, 2014). The drug epidemic is not only the use of illegal street drugs but prescription drugs, as the following charts from the National Institute on Drug Abuse will show.

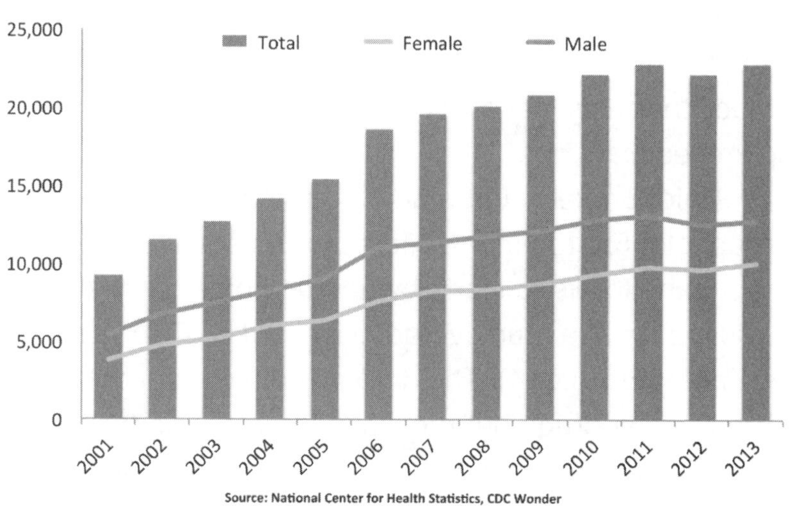

National Overdose Deaths—Number of Deaths from **Prescription Drugs.** The figure above is a bar chart showing the total number of US overdose deaths involving opioid prescription drugs from 2001 to 2013. The chart is overlaid by a line graph showing the number of deaths by females and males. From 2001 to 2013 there was a 2.5-fold increase in the total number of deaths.

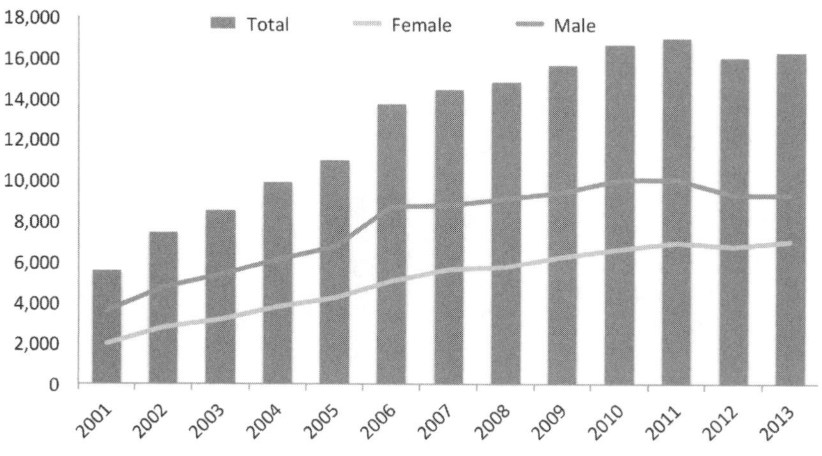

National Overdose Deaths—Number of Deaths from **Rx Opioid Pain Relievers.** The figure above is a bar chart showing the total number of US overdose deaths involving opioid pain relievers from 2001 to 2013. The chart is overlaid by a line graph showing the number of deaths by females and males. From 2001 to 2013 there was a 3-fold increase in the total number of deaths.

National Overdose Deaths

Number of Deaths from Benzodiazepines

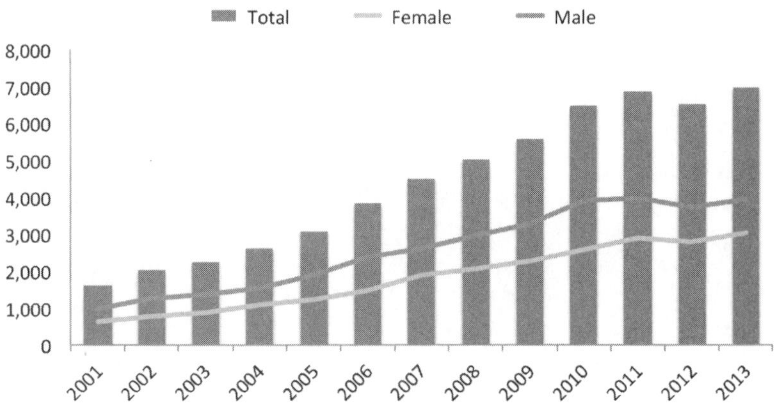

Source: National Center for Health Statistics, CDC Wonder

National Overdose Deaths — Number of Deaths from **Benzodiazepines.** The figure above is a bar chart showing the total number of US overdose deaths involving benzodiazepines from 2001 to 2013. The chart is overlaid by a line graph showing the number of deaths by females and males. From 2001 to 2013 there was a 4-fold increase in the total number of deaths.

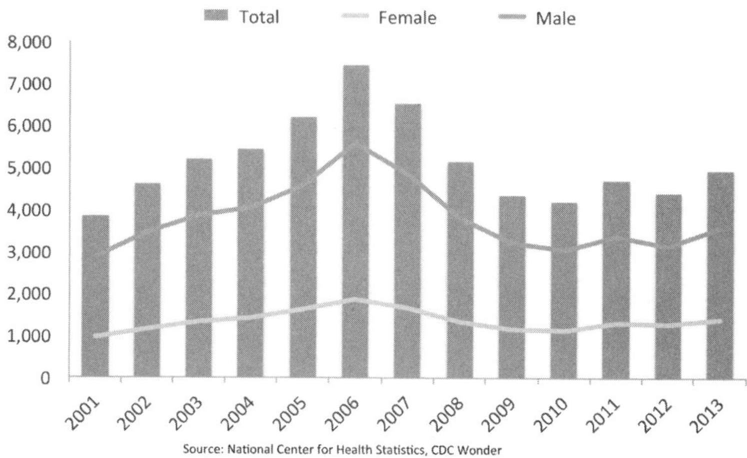

National Overdose Deaths—Number of Deaths from **Cocaine.** The figure above is a bar chart showing the total number of US overdose deaths involving cocaine from 2001 to 2013. The chart is overlaid by a line graph showing the number of deaths by females and males. From 2001 to 2013 there was a 29% increase in the total number of deaths.

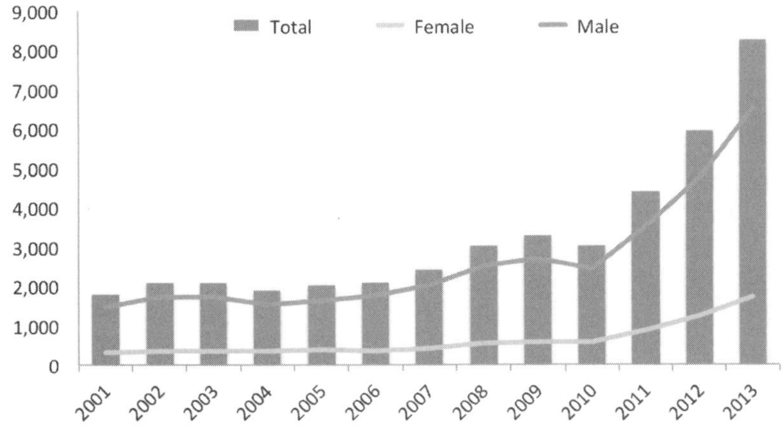

National Overdose Deaths—Number of Deaths from **Heroin.** The figure above is a bar chart showing the total number of US overdose deaths involving heroin from 2001 to 2013. The chart is overlaid by a line graph showing the number of deaths by females and males. From 2001 to 2013 there was a 5-fold increase in the total number of deaths.

Is there HOPE for the addict? Is there an answer for addiction's tight grip? Is there a power stronger than the power of addiction? Can YOU or your loved one become FREE from the control of addiction and live a productive life? **Absolutely yes!**

When Paul the Apostle asked his rhetorical question, "Who shall deliver me from this terrible state that I am in?" He answered it with, "Thank God! The answer is in Jesus Christ our Lord. So you see how it is: In my mind I really want to obey God's law, but because of my sinful nature I am a slave to sin." (Romans 7:25 NLB)

He is the One who can free those trapped. He is stronger than any addiction! **There is a higher power... His name is Jesus Christ!** At Teen Challenge New England & New Jersey we have a 15-month residential program that has proven to work again and again because of the "Jesus factor." He is the central focus; who can and does break the power of addiction. The program is designed to assist the student in dealing with issues and re-entering back into society as a productive healthy person. But our success rate would not be what it is without each addict forming a personal relationship with Jesus Christ.

This past year we started an "End Addiction" Campaign to educate and bring a greater awareness to the dangers of addiction. We have placed billboards, printed literature, and produced wristbands, pens and banners to raise awareness and promote the campaign. We are bringing this campaign into schools to help young people learn about the dangers of drugs and alcohol. You can join us in our fight to "End Addiction" one person at a time by donating at our website www.tcnewengland.org today!

This is the second book in a series called *"Changed Lives," Ten True Stories from Addiction to Freedom.* These stories represent people who were once held captive by the power of addiction but are now set FREE! These stories prove that Teen Challenge New England & New Jersey can and does change lives. The people in the stories recognize that Jesus is the Son of God, can give new life, and what He taught in the Bible is central to the process.

I trust that as you read this book you will be touched by the stories and that they will bring HOPE to you and your loved ones who may be ensnared in the trap of addiction.

Chapter 1
The History of Teen Challenge New England & New Jersey

Thomas Parker

Why The Name Teen Challenge?

For many years people have asked, "Why is the name of our organization 'Teen Challenge' when the majority of those who enter our centers are adults?" The answer is simple and really quite miraculous. In his book, *The Cross and the Switchblade*, David Wilkerson, the pastor of a little mountain church in Pennsylvania describes how he was sitting in his study one evening in 1958 reading an article in Life magazine. The article was about seven teenaged gang members who were on trial for murdering a handicapped boy in New York City. Although initially revolted by the brutality and senselessness of the story, Brother Dave was dumbfounded by a thought that sprang into his head as though it had come into him from somewhere else. "Go to New York City and help those boys." While the trial was still in progress, he went by faith and once there, he began to see the dramatic manifestations of New York's teenage gang members: violence, sex and drug addiction. But God put a dream in his heart, "They've got to start over again, and they've got to be surrounded by love." And so what began initially as Teen Age Evangelism on the streets of New York soon developed into Brother Dave's vision of a home where teenage gang members and drug addicts who needed special help could come into an atmosphere of discipline and affection and be renewed by the same love that he had watched on the streets in Teen Age Evangelism.

Then, in late December, 1960, Teen Challenge Center was opened in Brooklyn, NY. As years went by and the drug epidemic increased, more and more people were coming into the growing number of Teen Challenge Centers. They were men and women in their 20's, 30's and even older who had wonderful potential, but were lost in a world of tragic waste. As Teen Challenge has grown for more than half a century, the name Teen Challenge has become famous all over the world and is still recognizable as the place where Jesus continues to change lives of teens and adults.

(Pentecostal Evangel, October 11, 1964)
"TEEN CHALLENGE IS LAUNCHED IN BOSTON"

In spite of the fact that they said, "It cannot be done in Boston", it is being done! Miracle after miracle of deliverance has taken place daily. Although Boston is known as an educational center with high cultural achievements, it is a city without a forceful gospel witness for the masses on the streets where prostitution, drug addiction and teen-age delinquency are rampant.

Stirred by the city's great spiritual need, a group of businessmen and pastors from the Boston area spent three days visiting the Teen Challenge Center in New York City to observe the great work God was doing there.

As a result of this challenge, they invited David Wilkerson, director of the New York Center, to help them initiate a center in the greater Boston area. Gayle F. Lewis, Executive Director of the Assemblies of God Home Missions, met with a committee and approved the new project.

> On June 12th over 600 interested friends and guests attended the kickoff rally banquet.

The committee soon purchased a building at 414 Jamaica Way in Jamaica Plain, Massachusetts and dedicated it to the Lord as the Boston Teen Challenge Center with Rev. David Milley as the Director. Twenty-one staff workers from various Bible colleges joined the summer staff.

(Pentecostal Evangel, August 27, 1967)
"TEEN CHALLENGE ON THE MOVE"

"Teen Challenge teams have spent the summer invading the ghetto sections and suburban neighborhoods. They intercept young people in the beach amusement areas, slum sections, thoroughfares, housing projects, and vice centers. They even go into the worst parts of the city, where policemen take dogs with them for protection. This type of approach is unique in Boston and many orthodox churchmen were shocked to find converted addicts and gang leaders standing on street corners singing and preaching. Contacts have been made with the underworld, with drug addicts and beatnik subcultures.

But the greatest impact is being demonstrated by the spiritual awakening that has taken place in a number of the denominational churches. Several thousand souls have been saved through these outreaches. The ministry of Teen Challenge in Boston has quickly become a demonstration of the Holy Ghost baptism in action."

Since its beginning in 1964, as the fourth Teen Challenge established in the United States, God has miraculously expanded the borders from Boston to all six New England states and New Jersey. From that small "mustard seed" beginning, the message of hope and freedom from addiction has been spreading to every addict in the region. We want to honor the many great leaders and staff, both past and present, for their contributions to this miraculous movement. Please follow with me now as we look back at some of the major events in the growth and expansion of Teen Challenge in New England.

In 1968:

• As the need grew for a larger facility to serve the growing number of addicts who were responding to God's transforming message, the Boston center closed and began to relocate to a new, larger campus in nearby Brockton, Massachusetts under such Executive Directors as Bob Beuscher and Jim Vitale.

In 1982:

• With no program in Boston due to the move to Brockton, a new men's center, Boston Outreach Ministries, was opened by Rodney Hart, a former graduate of the Teen Challenge Training Center in Rehrersburg, Pennsylvania.

In 1989:

• Soon after opening the second men's center located in Providence, Rhode Island, Rodney Hart answered God's call to become an Assembly of God Missionary in Paraguay, South America. Bob Strothoff, another graduate of the Teen Challenge Training Center in Rehrersburg, Pennsylvania, was chosen as the new Executive Director over both centers and Boston Outreach Ministries became Outreach Ministries, Inc.

• Our current president, Pasco A. Manzo served as Chairman of the Board of Outreach Ministries, Inc. for ten years.

In 1992:

• Outreach Ministries Inc. received official accreditation as a Teen Challenge organization by the Southern New England District of the Assemblies of God (SNED) and Teen Challenge USA (TCUSA), and was now Outreach Ministries, Inc. Teen Challenge.

In 1994:

• After 17 years of faithfully waiting and trusting the Lord to fulfill his promise to her, Jacqui Strothoff opened the Restoration Home for Women in Providence, Rhode Island as the third Teen Challenge center in Outreach Ministries, Inc. Teen Challenge.

In 1996:

• Floyd Miles, the Dean of Men at Teen Challenge Ministry Center Brockton and founder of The Harvest

House re-entry program for Teen Challenge graduates, opened the Teen Challenge Connecticut men's campus in New Haven, Connecticut.

In 1997:

• Tom Parker, the former Program Director of Boston Outreach and Outreach Ministries, Inc. Teen Challenge, became the Executive Director of Outreach Ministries, Inc. Teen Challenge.

In 1999:

• Rodney Hart, returning from the mission field in South America, was appointed as the Executive Director of Teen Challenge Ministry Center Brockton.

• Then, in an unprecedented decision, the Executive Directors of these three separately incorporated Teen Challenge organizations in Brockton, New Haven and Boston/Providence merged into one unified organization, Teen Challenge New England, Inc. Their decision was made in an effort to unite and develop Teen Challenge throughout New England and reach every addict with the message of hope and freedom from addiction by the life changing power of Jesus Christ. And God's floodgates began to open!

"You have gained glory for yourself;
you have extended all the borders of the land."
Isaiah 26:15b

In 2000:

• Teen Challenge New Hampshire men's campus in Manchester was opened and is currently under the leadership of Executive Director Steve Gadomski.

In 2001:

• The Brockton, Massachusetts Thrift Store opened and is currently under the leadership of Director Oscar Cruz.

In 2002:

• The New Haven, Connecticut Thrift Store opened and is currently under the leadership of Executive Director Rick Welch.

In 2004:

• A unique opportunity arose when Teen Challenge was invited to minister to the inmates on a daily basis inside the Dartmouth House of Correction in Dartmouth, Massachusetts as an outreach for Teen Challenge admissions.

• Teen Challenge Boston, currently under the leadership of Associate Director Jonathan Mello, expands and purchases a second home in Dorchester, Massachusetts.

In 2005:

• Teen Challenge Vermont men's campus in Johnson was opened and is currently under the leadership of Executive Director Rick Welch.

In 2006:

• Teen Challenge Brockton, currently under the leadership of Director Oscar Cruz completes its men's dormitory expansion from a 70 man capacity to over a 100 man capacity.

• Teen Challenge New Hampshire expands its dormitory capacity by purchasing a second home for staff and student housing.

• Teen Challenge Boston expands again and purchases a third home in Dorchester, Massachusetts.

In 2007:

• God gifted Teen Challenge with nearly 485 acres in Winthrop, Maine and Teen Challenge Maine men's campus was opened and is currently under the leadership of Associate Director Keith LaFleur.

• Teen Challenge New Jersey men's campus was opened in Newark and is currently under the leadership of Director Todd Sheehan.

• Teen Challenge Vermont expands its dormitory capacity by purchasing a second home for staff and student housing.

• Teen Challenge Rhode Island women's campus expands its dormitory capacity by purchasing a second home for staff and student housing.

• The Fitchburg Adolescent Girls' Teen Challenge opened in Fitchburg MA under the leadership of Executive Director Jacqui Strothoff and Associate Director Apryl Cordry. It was the first Teen Challenge adolescent girl's home in New England.

In 2008

• Under the leadership of Dr. Rodney Hart, focus was given to Teen Challenge Puerto Rico in an effort to assist them in bringing about their financial stability and developing programmatic structure.

In 2009:

• During the next 5 years, focus was given to providing staff, training and stability to the new and existing Teen

Challenge Centers in New England and New Jersey, and to their enterprises.

In 2014:

• Pasco A. Manzo was appointed as the President of Teen Challenge New England, Inc. Pasco had faithfully served for ten years (1989-1999) as the Chairman of the Board of Directors of Outreach Ministries, Inc. Teen Challenge and on the Board of Directors for Teen Challenge New England since 2007. Under Pasco Manzo's leadership the following was accomplished:

• God did another huge miracle in August and gifted Teen Challenge New Jersey with 88 acres with 22 buildings in Clinton Township near Lebanon. Our student capacity will increase to 100 beds and allow us to reach even more addicts in New Jersey and the surrounding areas.

• The publication of Changed Lives – Book One – Ten True Stories: From Addiction to Freedom. Over 6,000 copies have been sold or given away.

• Long needed renovations in the Corporate Headquarters building, including offices, kitchen and bathrooms, were started in 2014 and completed in 2015.

In 2015:

• The recently renovated Community Hope Center was opened in Brockton, Massachusetts. This venue holds up to 175 people and is available to all outside organizations for banquets, meetings and other program events.

• God did another huge miracle and gifted Teen Challenge New Hampshire with a 32,000 square foot building and lot in Nashua, New Hampshire. A Teen Challenge thrift store was opened in May 2015 and the building also serves as a Crisis Referral Center to help even more people in need.

• The Corporate Headquarters multi-purpose auditorium along with the foyer, learning center, dining room and bathrooms was completely renovated in Brockton, Massachusetts. This auditorium holds up to 700 people and is used for Teen Challenge graduations, banquets and other program events.

• The Teen Challenge transition house, "The Rivers Edge" opened in New Haven, Connecticut. This transition house is to provide structure, accountability and spiritual mentoring for Teen Challenge graduates and other qualified individuals in the process of rebuilding their lives and growing in their relationship with God.

• In March, a Teen Challenge satellite office was opened

in New London, Connecticut.

• *517Furniture* a division of the Teen Challenge Brockton Thrift store was opened. Donated furniture is repaired, restored and repurposed providing income for Teen Challenge and job skills for students.

• In June the *Aftercare Planning and Development* program was implemented. The program consists of relapse prevention, resume writing, computer access, employment investigation, missions and ministry resources, college application, church selection, financial studies and more.

• In June, July and August Teen Challenge Rhode Island was on Block Island conducting outreaches and raising awareness of the Teen Challenge program.

• As the need grows for a larger facility to serve the growing number of adult women struggling with addiction, preparations are being made to relocate the Women's Teen Challenge in Providence, Rhode Island. A larger site will not only serve the growing number of adult women, but will also provide the space to include their children as well!

God is on the move here in New England & New Jersey. In spite of the fact that they said, "It cannot be done in Boston," over 50 years ago, it was done and it continues to be done. Miracle after miracle of "Changed Lives" are taking place throughout New England & New Jersey, and we are trusting God for even more in the years to come so that every addict will know that there is HOPE in Jesus Christ!

Make no mistake about it, it is not Teen Challenge that changes the lives and hearts of the men and women who come through our doors, it is Jesus Christ. Catherine B. Hess from the National Institute of Mental Health, in her Research Summation, conducted a 7 year study (1968-1975) to find out if the 70% success rate that was claimed by Teen Challenge was accurate. Her findings showed that it was not 70%, but 86%. What made Teen Challenge different from all other programs came to be known as **"The Jesus Factor."**

During all of these years, God has continued to bless us and guide us along every step of this journey that has resulted in literally thousands of "Changed Lives" by the preaching of the Gospel message and the power of the Holy Spirit.

Thank you so much for partnering with us through this miraculous journey and for your faithful prayers and continued support. May the Lord Bless you all as you read these new stories of "Changed Lives"!

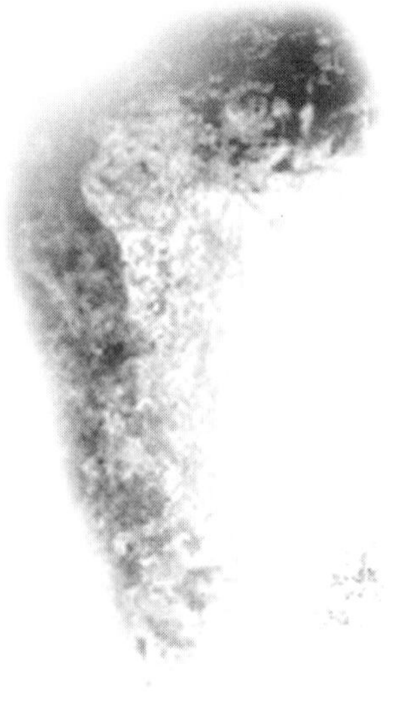

Chapter 2
A Knock on the Door

Lloyd Alcon

I am one of many who have been set free from addiction and a life of concealed inner torment. Like those before me, I suffered a whole lot of pain before I would find a whole lot of love to replace it. Those that have suffered much, greatly appreciate God's salvation. The depths of despair are a sharp contrast to the heightened blessing of God's grace.

The quote, "Sometimes it's not about the destination, but the journey itself" rings so true for the story of my life. Without the journey, I might never have found what I was seeking or have been saved by my Lord and Savior, Jesus Christ.

For all of you who have walked this walk, you will recognize the truths of my story. For all those still seeking, I pray that it may help you on the journey to freedom and peace found in Jesus Christ.

Early On

I was born November 1956 in Hoboken, New Jersey. I was one of four siblings and my parents were Cuban immigrants who came to America in December 1951. My father went to school and was a highly educated man who worked very hard pursuing his dream of having a good job, being successful and raising his family in the way any proud Cuban father would have.

Occasionally he would bring me to his New York office at First National City Bank (later to become Citibank). I would dress up in my suit and tie, just like him. Everything about my dad, the glamour surrounding his job, seemed so important and official. After our time at the bank, we would go to Times Square for lunch at a bar and grill. He would give me some change and I would go to the arcade next door to play games. When it was time to go, I remember my dad acted differently when we left the bar, but I didn't think much about it, I loved being with my dad.

Things changed as he drank more and more. I remember lots of yelling and arguing between him and my mom. His drinking took a toll on the whole family and I developed a nervous facial twitch, blinking and squinting hard. The abuse and the uncertainty affected everyone in the family and I was always afraid that something bad was going to happen to one of us.

My dad lost his job at the bank because of his drinking, and became unemployed for a year. My mother went to work in factories, and we all chipped in to support the household. I earned money delivering papers and milk for the Dellwood Milk Company. When I was twelve years old, my mom and dad separated.

Afterwards, my father still lived in town, and we were always worried that we would run into him drunk and there would be an embarrassing scene. In 1975, however, he left and moved to El Paso Texas. I never saw my father again and by this time, I felt accountable to no one.

Innocence Lost

At twelve years old, I sought an escape from my home life and turned to the streets. Cigarettes, alcohol and marijuana were readily available and I liked how they provided me a detachment from reality. During my teenage years I had lots of friends and within my larger group, there was a smaller group that was my closest friends. Although even with our closeness, I couldn't tell them what happened to me one night, coming out of a teen club hangout, called The Open Ear.

That night I was taken by force and sexually assaulted. I was high at the time and easy prey for a predator. I couldn't believe or understand why this would happen to me and I felt so much shame and guilt. I couldn't tell anyone—and I do mean no one—what had happened for fear of what else would happen to me. I had seen firsthand how friends, even close friends, can be very cruel.

So I told no one and as a result both my head and my heart wanted to explode.

I felt so trapped and the only way I knew how to escape such pain was with alcohol and drugs.

I was around 14 year old when I first took LSD (Lysergic acid diethylamide). Now I really was a mess inside, a third realm of non-reality. Talk about escaping, I loved the feeling this hallucinogen gave me. I began taking all different kinds of acid, THC (Tetrahydrocannabinol), mescaline; my menu of escape drugs grew and grew.

Music was a huge part of my life and that coincided with the drug use. I loved listening to music and playing music—drums, guitar, and singing. Washington Square Park and the Academy of Music were my favorite places to hang out. Anything and everything to satisfy my desires was found there. Even with the music and the drugs, inside, I was always insecure and never felt good enough, constantly trying to impress others and fit in. Relationships with girls were always difficult. My inner pain was suppressed, yet it was still molding me all the time. I couldn't get rid of the shame I felt and all that came with it.

Into the Fire

I married my childhood sweetheart right after high school on January 23, 1976. My daughter was born one month later. This wasn't really what I had planned for my life, to be married with a child, I loved them but I was also terrified. How was I going to do this? However, I embraced the huge responsibility and did the best I could. It made me proud to have something I could call my own: the love I had for my daughter and wife.

I continued to use drugs and alcohol because I was young and believed I deserved it. Drug and alcohol use were a huge part of the 70's culture. Overall, the 70's were a weird time of life, the turmoil of witnessing the events of the Vietnam War, government unrest, racism, riots, economic uncertainty made for a fragile future. It was terrifying as a new father, wondering what the future would hold, not alone, but with a family to provide for. Soon I had another child to support when my son was born in 1979.

My goal was to get a solid job, so I became a firefighter. I passed the written and a physical endurance test. This was a real job with a future and I worked hard to get there. Unfortunately, in this line of work, alcoholism was very prevalent and drug use was present as well, but more hidden.

It soon became apparent to me that I was a functioning addict. I continued to use but I was good at my job. I received a Class 3 citation for demonstrating unusual personal risk saving a mother and her children and on another occasion, saving the lives of fellow firefighters. Despite the excitement of the job, and the enormous weight of responsibility that came with it, I became complacent about using while on duty, and my shame and guilt were compounded. Alcohol and cocaine continued to be a part of my life, but eventually it got out of control, and then I was introduced to crack cocaine. Wow, did that hit the spot, the empty spot. But it really wasn't empty at all; this was the spot where my shame and pain hid.

The difference with crack cocaine was the physical addiction and mental euphoria it provided. This was the start of my downfall. The physical addiction was overtaken by the psychological need to relive that first tsunami of pleasure. I never got it back, but I kept chasing it. Full addiction had taken me prisoner—there was no escape. Reality no longer existed, I was hooked.

> This new addiction became a full-blown affair, as I was trying to escape my past and inner pain.

I was so mad at myself, and it was so sad. All the time

I had told myself, "Don't wind up like dad." Yet still, I had become what I despised.

Eventually, all the help offered me had failed. I felt unreachable inside and hopeless. I was losing everything and everyone around me. I couldn't feel anything anymore. The importance and urgency of everything was gone. Reality was slipping away very fast. The love for those in my life was overtaken by the love of my addiction. My wife had divorced me and my daughter went to live with her boyfriend. She was in college, but I couldn't pay her tuition. Even now, I can't believe I did and felt such things. An eviction notice was nailed to my door, my car had been repossessed, and my family was gone. My desire was to love, but my will to do so was gone. I had zero, there was nothing left. I was at my lowest point.

Divine Intervention

My final effort to escape was attempted suicide. I was ready to jump off my balcony, when I heard a knock on the door. I thought it might be a drug dealer that I owed money to and if I opened the door, I would die instead by a gunshot. I ran to the door, glad that the pain would finally be over. Instead of a drug dealer, there stood an out-of-breath reverend that lived in my building. I exclaimed, "Reverend Cletti, what are you doing here?" He answered, "You tell me, Lloyd. God sent me up here."

I collapsed on the floor and felt an overwhelming presence of peace. He proceeded to explain to me how my pain could stop, and said, "You need Jesus. There's a place you can go to get help. It's called Teen Challenge. Don't be afraid. There are many people from different walks of life who are getting help: police, firemen, doctors, and others who have found salvation and freedom from the bondage of addiction." To this day, the sound of a knock on a door has become my endearing moniker of God's saving grace. It always reminds me of that moment on the balcony when I felt God in my heart telling me, "Not this one, I have a plan for you."

Because of the love and compassion of my fire chief, I was able to have excused time from my job and enter into the Teen Challenge program. As he put it, "You're a good man Lloyd, get the help you need." So began the journey of becoming whole again. In the summer of 1999, I entered Teen Challenge Brooklyn, New York. The roots of my restoration began at the very site of the birth of Teen Challenge, founded by Reverend David Wilkerson in 1958. Here I accepted Jesus Christ as my Lord and Savior. Then in the fall, I transferred to Teen Challenge Connecticut. God really began to take hold of me there. But it was hard for me to submit, mainly because of the process I had to go through. It was here that I met Rick Welch, currently Executive Director of Teen Challenge Connecticut and Teen Challenge Vermont. He was my mentor and he explained to me how to understand faith, and what would have to occur to transform me.

He told me how much God loved me, and wanted to give me a life that I had never experienced before. I'm not talking about a material life, but the inner life I needed, without the innermost parts where all the pain and mistrust lived. I had lived with this pain because it was all I had ever really known and didn't know that it could be healed.

Our time together brought out how similar our life stories were. I trusted him. I had finally found someone who knew my pain and would not judge me, he accepted me and loved me for who I was; just how Jesus sees me, and wants me to become the person He wants me to be. I learned to understand what forgiveness meant, and how I could have a new heart, bringing me a new life.

Jesus being the perfect Son of God was willing to receive me for who I was, with all my pain and shame. He wanted to take it from me and free me from my own condemnation. Accepting His gift of salvation and allowing Him to be my personal Savior was by far the most important and rewarding decision of my life.

I graduated the program and went back to New Jersey against the advice of Rick Welch. I returned to my fire chief and my fire company. I continued to do well for a while, but after about a year, I returned to my old lifestyle. This was a detrimental choice, especially after tasting and knowing the goodness of the Lord. Returning to my old life brought me close to another brush with death because my dealer was coming to kill me. I had to, literally, run for my life.

Teen Challenge New England & New Jersey has a seven month restoration program for graduates that have fallen back into addiction. While talking to Richard Welch and trying to lie about my circumstances to my best friend, he said, "When you feel like telling me the truth, call me back." Immediately I did. I told him the truth, and he told me to pack a bag and get to Teen Challenge in New Haven, Connecticut. I knew in my heart I had to return, surrender my career as a firefighter, and devote the rest of my life in servant hood to my Savior, Jesus Christ. This was the true turning point of my life.

Vermont Vision

After completing the restoration program, Rick asked me to join him in establishing a Teen Challenge in Vermont where men in addiction could get help. After the invitation, and much prayer, God spoke to my heart to go to Vermont because I knew people there were dying from addiction. It was the first solid indication of where my servant hood would begin. I knew this would be my calling. I think of Isaiah 61:1-2, which speaks of how the Lord authorized Isaiah to go to Israel and proclaim freedom to the Jews in Babylon. I felt God was placing a similar calling on my life; to go to Vermont and free the captives of addiction through Jesus Christ. I would let God use my life as an example that you can be changed and renewed when one surrenders their will. In my firefighting career I had physically saved lives, and now I was being called by the Lord to continue to help save lives, and souls, through the ministry of Teen Challenge.

Over the course of two years, we started to build the financial base that would be needed to open and sustain a Teen Challenge center. We began with drug awareness education and fundraising, and Sunday choir ministries where love offerings were collected from the many churches we visited on a weekly basis. Soon we were receiving students in the program and sending them to other Teen Challenge centers throughout New England until we established a permanent home in Vermont.

After traveling the length and breadth of the state, we were miraculously directed to the future Vermont site by an invitation to breakfast with a pastor who owned property in Johnson, Vermont. This would indeed be our new home, from which God would pour His grace upon the addicted and spiritually lost in Vermont. Their cries had been heard.

Before us was what seemed to be an insurmountable task. There were many needs: repairs to the property, the physical equipment and staff to make the property functional, and most of all, the money to pay for it all. But God was faithful and Teen Challenge Vermont opened its doors on January 3, 2005. Richard Stewart was our first intake student, and he is on staff today, still supporting the program!

Anniversary Milestone

This year we celebrated our tenth anniversary doing God's work of changing lives to nearly 1,000 men who have passed through our doors. Hallelujah!

From our meager beginnings and what little we had to offer, we have built upon the foundation of what the ministry offered; freedom and a changed life. God has multiplied our efforts so that many more could come to receive help, healing, and HOPE!

Looking back at what we faced, and what had to be accomplished, this could not have been done by mere men. It could only be done through the power of God. And it will always be a God-thing, the transforming power of Jesus Christ at work to change lives.

I have finally realized after many years of attempting to suppress the desire to truly feel whole, loved and wanted, that it was Christ who had always been there, extending his hand of mercy, but I never reached for it. I had reached for many other things before, but never his hand until I found Teen Challenge. Since then, my life purpose has been to help others in the same way Christ helped me, being an extension of his kingdom, being his disciple, and to disciple others.

The journey continues…
Amen

Chapter 3
Drunk Then, Director Now

Steve Gadomski

My name is Stephen Gadomski and I'm 55 years old. I have been sober for 25 years. I was raised in a home with hard working parents who loved me. Unfortunately, my parents liked to drink and party on the weekends, often hosting several drinking parties for their friends. When my parents were intoxicated, they would physically and verbally abuse each other. I grew up in an environment filled with tension, violence and drunkenness. I always thought that our family was like every other. However, the older I got and the more I observed my friend's families, I realized that my family was far from normal.

The Adolescent Years

Both of my parents worked full time jobs and my dad also worked a part time job on the weekends, so quality time with my parents was limited. My dad also did two tours in Vietnam; consequently his influence in my life was little to none. I filled my adolescent years with football, baseball, and track and field. My parents did occasionally attend some of my sporting events. Unfortunately, the violence at home continued to escalate. My parents continued to fight, separated, divorced, remarried and divorced again. This time in my life was so chaotic; I witnessed many terrifying things and was scared.

Stephen's Journey to Addiction

My dysfunctional childhood set the stage for my addiction. I had some painful memories and hurt that needed healing. I started experimenting with alcohol at 13 years old and had an instant love for how it made me feel. Soon I began to lose interest in sports and instead every weekend I would hang out with my buddies and get drunk. At 16 years old, I was introduced to marijuana. I was living with my mother, Barbara, and her boyfriend who would eventually become my step-father George. I wasn't happy living with my mother and her unreasonable rules, so I left and went to live with my father. He soon abandoned me and I was on my own. Every weekend my apartment was where all my friends would gather for drinking parties. Between school, part time work, and the drinking, drug infested weekends; financially I was barely making ends meet. At one point, I couldn't pay the rent, there was no food in the house and my car had broken down. One day at a pay phone, in the pouring rain, I called my mother and pleaded with her to let me come back home. Her answer shocked and hurt me deeply, she said that, "I had made my choice and there was no way she would let me come back home." As I hung up the phone, I realized she was right and I decided that I would have to fend for myself.

Stephen's Adult Life

At 17 years old my alcohol and drug use increased into an everyday occurrence. I became very resentful towards my mother and father and cut them both out of my life. The only stability and love I had in my life was my girlfriend Noreen. I dropped out of high school and began to work full time. My life became filled with work, partying, and hanging out with my friends. I had become head over heels in love with Noreen who was also caught up in this lifestyle of partying. The company I was working for transferred me to Portland, Maine. Noreen and I agreed to stay together and see each other on the weekends. Not long after my transfer to Maine I proposed to Noreen and she accepted.

> Those years of separation and my loneliness added to my alcohol and drug abuse.

I was working third shift and was medicating myself to go to sleep and to work.During this time, I discovered methamphetamines, we called it speed or crank. I was smoking marijuana, eating Quaaludes, and drinking myself to sleep, while eating black beauties (meth) like jelly beans to stay awake at night. My life became a rollercoaster ride Monday through Friday and the weekends were a drinking party blowout. Soon I became a hallucinogenic junky and fell in love with acid and magic mushrooms taking many trips with my friends. Later I was also introduced to cocaine and freebasing. I experimented with many different drugs during these years.

Life with Noreen

Noreen and I were married by the time I was twenty on November 24, 1979 and we began our life together as husband and wife. I transferred back to Nashua, New Hampshire and continued working for the same company. Noreen found work in the service industry and we moved into our first apartment. By this time my addiction was out of control, I drank and did drugs daily and Noreen wasn't far behind. My addiction led me into a time of disrespecting authority and getting into trouble with the law. I was constantly getting into accidents with motor vehicles and acquired numerous DUI and driving without a license convictions. This led to times of incarceration, loss of driving privileges, and finally a ten year to indefinite suspension of my driver's license. It was a very turbulent time in our lives. Noreen would have to drive me to work and pick me up. I was a full blown alcoholic, and addicted to cocaine but living in denial. Noreen had her own issues with marijuana and alcohol as well. Those early years of our marriage were a blur of adventure and tragedy.

The Miracle of Changed Lives

Our friends began to marry and move away from the party lifestyle, while my addiction continued to escalate; I was showing up to work drunk and high. Then one of my best friends Rick received Christ as his personal Lord and Savior. Rick began to witness to my wife Noreen on the phone. I would come home from work and Noreen would tell me everything that they had talked about. She thought he was crazy. She told me how he was all fired up about his new life and how God had changed him. Rick offered to fly me and Noreen out to Texas, an all-expense paid trip. All he asked of us was to attend a church service with him on Sunday morning, so Noreen and I agreed to go. We figured we would at least get a free vacation. Rick picked us up at the airport and immediately you could tell there was something different about him.

> This wasn't the same man I drank and did drugs with. He glowed with the glory of God and he smiled all the time.

Noreen was instantly interested and Rick was filled with excitement about Jesus, his Savior, and talked about Him constantly. I continued drinking alcohol all the way up to Sunday morning church service. The church was packed with about 3,000 people and the place was going nuts with worship music. It was unlike any church I had ever been to in my life. The pastor finished his sermon and asked if anyone wanted to receive Christ as their personal Savoir. Noreen and I lifted our hands, got to our feet and ran to the altar. Noreen and I received Christ on September 22, 1982 and the pastor encouraged us about what to do with the new life Jesus Christ had given us. For the remainder of our time with Rick, he encouraged us and took us to church services and prayer meetings. I stopped drinking that whole week.

Returning Home

Coming home was exciting. Right away we found a church where we could worship and told all our friends what had happened to us. We told them all about Jesus and how he changed our lives and we had no desire to drink or get high anymore. Our friends of course were concerned about us and a little resistant of our enthusiasm about Jesus Christ. It didn't take long before my friend's taunting and ridicule wore me down and I began to drink again. Noreen was disappointed in me and told me that I could do what I wanted, but she had found what she had been looking for her whole life. Our church and other Christians reached out to me, but I didn't want anything to do with the Christian way of life. I knew something had happened to me, but I didn't quite understand it all. Within a matter of months, I was sucked back into my addiction. Things became even worse than before and I began a seven year journey of hell on earth as I backslid away from my new life in Christ. Noreen and I started a family and our first daughter Samantha was born on August 4, 1983. I thought having a family would help settle me down but my addiction became worse. I promised Noreen if she had another baby I would stop drinking and our second daughter Katherine was born on September 21, 1987. Of course I broke my promise and continued in my addition. Alcohol and cocaine consumed my life to the point of risking everything that was dear to me; my job, my marriage, my children and even my life.

A Dramatically Changed Life

I had no hope of ever having a life apart from drugs and alcohol. During this time God was dealing with my heart, but I didn't know how to get back the feeling I experienced in that church service so long ago in Texas. Noreen tolerated years of verbal abuse and neglect during those seven years when I was away from God. My misery came to a stop one evening. High and drunk at home, the phone rang. I answered the phone and it was one of Noreen's girlfriends from church. The joy in her voice pierced me like a knife and I yelled for Noreen. "It's your %*#! friend from your &*#! church." Noreen came to the phone and asked if she could call her friend back in a few minutes. Noreen looked at me and said "You're a miserable person aren't you?" Something inside me broke and I began to cry and yell. "Yes, I am miserable, but I don't know what to do." Noreen and I went back and forth for hours talking. There was a spiritual battle going on for my soul. Noreen said, "You need to pray with me and invite Jesus back into your life."

We prayed together and I could feel the love of God embracing me and restoring me back to life.

After Noreen and I were finished praying, I felt like a huge weight was lifted off of me. The look on Noreen's face as she gazed into my eyes shocked me. I asked her what was wrong, and she said, "Go look in the mirror." As I did, my countenance was changed; it was bright and I wasn't high or intoxicated any more. The joy that flooded my heart and soul was inexpressible and I just began to thank God for what He had done. I was able to share what had happened with many of my friends and family and they too saw the dramatic change in my life. Church attendance, Bible study and prayer became a regular routine in my life and I would never return to my life of addiction. That was on March of 1989 and I have never looked back.

Called to Change Lives

I felt God wanted me to begin a Teen Challenge in New Hampshire and I began to reach out to those I knew who were still addicted. I began to study to become a minister and started to visit a local Teen Challenge in Brockton, Massachusetts for some training. During those years Noreen and I had two more daughters, Kelly, born December 5, 1991 and then Elizabeth, born November 2, 1993. That year I would receive my Ministerial Credentials with the Assembly of God. During this time, I would travel to churches in New England sharing my desire to see a Teen Challenge residential drug and alcohol treatment center established in New Hampshire. We opened a crisis referral center in Manchester to reach out to addicts to try to get them into a Teen Challenge in another state. I started a Christian 12-step program out of our church's basement and began to serve in the prison system in New Hampshire. In 1998, we opened the first residential Teen Challenge in Nashua, New Hampshire. In 2000, we merged with the centers in Brockton, Boston, Connecticut, and Rhode Island to form Teen Challenge New England. In 2003, in order to increase bed capacity, we purchased the current home of Teen Challenge New Hampshire in Manchester. In 2015, God brought us back to our Nashua roots through the donation of a property that has become a Teen Challenge New Hampshire Thrift store and outreach center. It has been an awesome privilege to be part of what God has done in the New England area, to reach addicts with the message of HOPE. My only desire is to see addicts changed by the power of Jesus Christ and to live productive lives, free from their addictions.

Chapter 4
From D.C. to T.C.

Chris Mello

In 1950, I was born in New Bedford, Massachusetts to a loving mother and father who raised five sons and three daughters. Now at 64 years old, memories of my childhood are filled with love, joy, peace, security and a sense of self-worth and belonging. These feelings and emotions were not just derived from my family, but also from my Cape Verdean community. The morals, values and disciplines I was raised with, molded me into the young man I became.

My parents, as well as the others in the community, were committed to strong family values; integrity, trustworthiness, sharing, caring, unconditional love and the protection and the welfare of one another were always a priority. My mother lovingly and sacrificially provided for our every-day needs. She raised our family in a way that demonstrated to me what true love was all about. We were well dressed and ate three home-cooked meals a day. My mother made sure we went to church every Sunday, we attended catechism classes every Wednesday and confession on Saturdays. She was also a disciplinarian. Strict rules and curfews were set and kept.

My father, a police lieutenant by profession, provided for the family financially. However, his character, image and his personification of what it meant to be a man left a huge imprint on my life; one that I am not sure he was aware of. The fact that he never finished high school caused him to make sure we succeeded academically. My father was also a very competitive and a skilled athlete, which in turn, gave his children the desire to be successful in athletics as well.

In the Beginning

As I reflect on my childhood, I can vividly see how both of my parents' characteristics became entwined in my identity. As the third oldest boy, I was rather shy and introverted, with a strong desire to be accepted by family and friends. I was protected from my brothers by my mother and protected from the boys in the community by my brothers. I also felt a strong sense of security and respect in my community because of who my father was. I remember everyone calling him Mr. Mello. Although respect was given toward the elders of the community, I felt my father was shown an even deeper level of respect. Whenever he came by the park, the older guys would stop gambling and the girls would talk about how handsome he was. My father treated everyone fairly and with respect; therefore I concluded in my mind that this is why he commanded that same respect.

My father's competitive athletic spirit rubbed off on my older brothers and naturally I followed their footsteps. In order to live up to the family's reputation, I became very disciplined and committed to practicing and improving my skillsets, even taking the opportunity to play against the older guys. I also made this decision because the guys my own age were drinking and smoking cigarettes.

This decision paid off and I was awarded the best athlete award in three sports in junior high school.

This discipline continued in high school where I started guard alongside my brother and ended my senior year one point shy of a state basketball championship.

Education was a focal point of mine as well and in 1968, I was accepted to Howard University in Washington, D.C. In my freshman year, as a walk on, I started on the varsity basketball team and earned a scholarship. I was determined to excel in my academics and continue my educational studies beyond an undergraduate degree. Through disciplined and committed study habits, I received an academic scholarship to the University of Massachusetts at Amherst where I achieved my MBA in 1973, at the age of 22. I went back to Washington, D.C. and had an illustrious and successful career as an Account Executive with Xerox and Digital Equipment Corporations for 15 years. The rewards were many, with multiple trips a year throughout the United States and the Caribbean Islands as well as purchasing my first home and a BMW at the age of 28. I was once told "it seems like everything you touch turns to gold."

Gold to Dust

Despite the fact that I had entered college having never smoked a cigarette or indulged in any drugs or alcohol, it would be my journey of drug and alcohol abuse that would begin to tear my life down. Desiring to fit in with my college classmates, I began to smoke marijuana. My teammates introduced me to heroin and my neighborhood friend introduced me to mescaline. I prided myself on the fact that I could control when and what type of drug I would use. After all, I was a very logical person!

When I entered corporate America, I found out that my coworkers and even the managers drank a lot of alcohol and used drugs. However, they used the so-called "rich man's drug" cocaine. Now I was doing cocaine, high-end marijuana (Thai sticks and Hawaiian buds) and indulging in alcohol. What I found out was that I had a much higher tolerance than everyone else and I convinced myself that I could achieve the same success in the work force as I had in college by being disciplined and in control of my usage. I had the drug use under control. I was able to function and be productive at my job as I was named District Account Representative of the year numerous times. Rather than spend a lot of my own money, I would fudge my weekly expense account to pay for drugs. However, the alcohol was a different story. Every team meeting was always held at a hotel ending with an open bar reception. Business lunches with customers would always include drinking. I would drink at clubs during the week which led me to become a blackout drinker.

Return Home

In 1987, my wife, son, daughter and I moved to Mashpee, Massachusetts. In 1991, I lost my job at Digital due to corporate downsizing. A year later, my wife took the kids and our dog Malcolm and returned to New Bedford, Massachusetts saying, "I'm letting go and letting God." Although I knew that my addiction played a big part of her leaving, twice I had been pronounced dead from a heroin overdose, I was still hurt because we had been together since we were 16 years old. Shortly afterwards, I lost the house in Washington, DC.

In 1992, I totaled my car almost losing my life, and had to undergo multiple surgeries. Unfortunately, I was prescribed morphine which I took for an extended period of time. My addiction quickly escalated to where I found myself in and out of eight detoxes and two six-month programs over the next seven years.

During this time, while still employed in the software industry, I was stealing from my wife, children, mother, sister and co-workers to support my addiction.

I knew that I was in serious trouble when I staked out one of the neighborhood bars and timed exactly when to burglarize it. I went as far as to put on a mask outside the back door ready to go in, until I broke down and cried as I could not believe the person I had become. It was right after the Thanksgiving of 1999, when my entire family, including nieces and nephews, called for a meeting to confront, intervene and pray for me to change my life.

He Makes All Things New

Two weeks later, I entered the doors of Teen Challenge Brockton and GOD filled me with HIS HOLY SPIRIT at chapel service on Friday, December 9th. I made a commitment to myself that I was going to study the Word of God with the same passion and intensity in which I obtained my MBA. It was at the nine month mark when I shared this scripture with the rest of the student body, "On with it and finish with the same zeal in that which you started and with the resources at hand." That became my declaration to finish the program. At the 14-month mark, I was asked to make a one year commitment to be the Admissions Coordinator. This decision was confirmed in my heart when I had an unexpected dinner at a seminar in Boston with the pastor of my church. He was the one who prayed with me at the altar the Sunday before I came into Teen Challenge. The next day at the seminar, a woman prayed with me in an angelic voice and told me that God wanted me to forget my former career and say "yes" to the new one HE has in store for me.

The decision was made and 14 years later no one has ever asked me how long I am staying at Teen Challenge. During these years as a servant of the Lord, I have witnessed many miraculous works at the hands of our Lord and Savior. My son, Jonathan, came into the program and we now serve side by side (You can read Jonathan's story in Chapter 7). In 2005 with Pastor Jimmy Lilley, we started the Teen Challenge Dartmouth House of Corrections (DHOC) prison program. I've been blessed to attend 168 Teen Challenge graduation ceremonies and hear how the Lord continues to change lives. God used me to conduct numerous outreaches, to preach in various settings in New Bedford and declare the Word of God at my mother's, father's and brother's funerals. By the grace of God, He has used me to touch thousands of lives through the teaching and preaching of His word. I am forever grateful for my daughter's forgiveness and allowing me to be a big part of my two granddaughter's lives. But the one that means the most to me, is the restoration of my relationship with my wife who sacrificed and loved me unconditionally.

How about you? Do you see yourself in my story? Are you a professional who seems to have it all together, yet are living a lie? Have you lost your way and are on the verge of losing it all? There is hope for a changed life. God can move you from one life to a better one. God did it in mine and He can do it in yours too!

Chapter 5
Never Give Up

Christine Caparelli

Recently, on my way home from work, I saw a girl holding a sign standing along side the exit ramp. I didn't bother reading what the sign said because I only noticed what she looked like. She was blonde, thin and young, a very pretty girl. This girl reminded me of myself, almost 18 years ago. In my younger days, pulling over to offer help to a girl on the streets was something I did regularly. I realized it had been quite a while since I had done that and I knew I had to do something but I wasn't sure what. I made a turn into a near by parking lot to concoct my plan. I knew I needed to move swiftly; I may only have seconds before she was picked up by a "date." I approached this young girl and asked her if we could talk. She declined my invitation to get into my car but said if I wanted to tell her about how she could get help, I could pull over and she would be willing to talk. Although she stated that she never gets in anyone's car, I knew this was a lie. The truth was that getting in my car would take up too much of her time and could mean missing out on a "better offer." As I pulled back around to meet her in a nearby parking lot, I noticed a very overweight, older man in a big white car, a Lincoln or some other kind of huge "mob-style" sedan. She looked at the man and signaled him to wait as she walked over to my SUV. My concerns about her disappearing had been confirmed; had I waited a few more seconds, the opportunity would have been missed. The opportunity for what? I still didn't know. What could I offer her? Would a "pep" talk, speech or lecture really make a difference? Surely this girl would have to be detoxed and admitted somewhere. Then she would have to find a long-term treatment center to experience any lasting change in her life. How would I accomplish all these tasks in just one encounter? Don't laugh; I know you've thought the same thing. As these thoughts raced through my head, any effort I could make seemed futile. But I had to do something. When she made it to my door, I realized that this girl, although visibly worn down by the streets, was a lot prettier that I first thought. In fact, she was strikingly beautiful. I had decided that I would just tell her my story; a very quick version, as I knew her time was precious.

I found myself looking directly into the eyes of a younger version of me. I began our conversation by asking her how old she was. Her answer was 23, which was just three years older than me when I got clean. I realized that I only had one thing to offer her. She needed hope and my very existence could be proof of that. I shared a brief version of the following testimony with her.

I started by telling her who I was. I am 38 years old, registered nurse, a pastor's wife and a mother of four, Ashley 22, Michael 13, Hannah 12, and Olivia 9. But this life has not always been my story.

My life began as an unwanted pregnancy. My parents were divorced by the time I was two years old. I was a quiet child, insecure and unsure of myself. From the age of nine years old I was raised in an Assembly of God church. This church worked very closely with drug addicts as well as our local Teen Challenge centers, though I'm not completely sure of all the ways this affected me. I saw a lot growing up and I do feel that in some ways I was desensitized to what being a drug addict actually means. It's possible it made me less judgmental or maybe it made me less afraid of becoming one.

> I do know one thing for sure; I had seen drug addicts set free so I knew it was possible. This knowledge was something that I carried with me for the rest of my life.

At some point in my preteens, I realized that drinking relieved my feelings of insecurity in social environments. Shortly thereafter, I discovered the same effect from smoking marijuana. Around this time I began suffering from panic attacks and would wake up in the middle of the night stricken with fear. I couldn't bear to sleep alone, so I would get into bed with by younger brother or sister. My brother, fourteen months younger than me, especially didn't appreciate this and thought I was crazy, but luckily he slept like a rock and most of the time my presence went unnoticed. The anxiety began to creep into my days and I soon realized that smoking marijuana helped that problem too. I could now go to parties and not feel socially awkward; light up a joint, relax and have fun. This is how it all began, innocent enough and probably even familiar to some people. However it didn't end there. I became pregnant when I was 14 and shortly afterwards suffered a miscarriage. I was in pain and no one understood. Although only a child myself, I had become a mother and lost my own child. Most people around me were relieved that I "got off the hook" by miscarrying, but I was very confused about my feelings and had no one to talk to. I even remember hearing the words, "Oh good, thank God," by a Christian adult I loved and respected. I did the only thing I thought would alleviate my inner turmoil; I got pregnant again. I think it was on purpose, but honestly I don't completely know. My 8-pound 5-ounce little girl was born when I was 15. I loved being a mother. I dressed her up and took her places. Everything revolved around her, or so I thought. There was still something broken inside of me. I continued to smoke marijuana and drink before and after my pregnancy and for a little while it was manageable. Then I remember having episodes of drinking alone during the day when I put my daughter down for a nap. During this time I would call my friends and they would notice, asking me "Are you drunk at two o'clock in the afternoon?" At the time I didn't see it as a problem because I was also making some progress with my life. I obtained my driver's license, earned a GED and married my daughter's father.

Unfortunately, about a year later my daughter's father and I separated. Single for the first time as an adult, I entered the party scene. Most of us were doing the same things everyone our age did, but I found I always felt the need to go a little further than anyone else.

I experimented with different drugs until one day I found my "true love." I am not referring to a new boyfriend; I found heroin.

All of a sudden nothing bothered me. I wasn't worried, scared, inferior or insecure. I was just high and at the time, that was good enough for me. I would do anything to maintain that feeling. It wasn't long before I developed a physical dependence. At that point I wasn't simply trying to stay high; I was trying to become "normal" and prevent withdrawal symptoms. I spent the next few years chasing my drug of choice. During that time, I had my affairs with cocaine and other drugs but my heroin addiction was a constant. At first, I did everything the guys did to get their drugs; selling my own stuff, maxing out my credit cards, shoplifting, breaking into houses, "borrowing" money I would never pay back, etc. I swore that I would never do the things I saw other girls do. I had a good reputation in that regard and intended to keep it that way, or so I thought. Eventually I did enough damage that I lost custody of my daughter. I tried to get clean and even at one point managed to get her back only to lose custody again. My failure as a mother was something that pushed me further into my addiction in an attempt to mask my pain and not face the reality of my destroyed life.

Sporadically I attended church services, partly looking for help and partly because my church was my home and where my family was. In times of desperation I threw myself at the altar crying out to God for help. Strangely enough, I carried with me an absolute belief that God could deliver a drug addict. I had seen it growing up in that church and I knew it was a reality. My question, however, was not could He but would He? I wanted to be zapped and changed in an instant, but all along somehow I knew that was not part of His plan.

I continued to evade the difficult choice that I knew I had to make; the choice to surrender my life and go into long term treatment, specifically at Teen Challenge. I am not suggesting that this is God's plan for every addict, but for me, I knew it was.

After I had lost more than I was willing to give up, I came to the end of my rope and surrendered to God's plan. The night I surrendered, I was in jail lying in my bottom bunk reading a book by the light coming through the window of the door. I was up all night because I couldn't sleep due to the withdrawals. The book was written by a man who was involved in criminal activity; a man who repeatedly tried and failed in surrendering his life to God. This man continued to have lapses into his older years but didn't stop coming back to God for help. At the beginning of each chapter was a scripture verse. God spoke to me through that book because if this man in his eighties could keep trying and never give up, then surely I could be delivered at the age of twenty. I decided at that moment that I would surrender to God's will and enter Teen Challenge and that no matter how many times I fell I would get back up. I entered the Restoration Home for Women (Outreach Ministries Inc./Teen Challenge. See, The History of Teen Challenge, Chapter 1) in Providence, Rhode Island as their first student twenty-one years ago, but I didn't stay to complete the program. After two more admissions to

Providence, I eventually entered the Walter Hoving Home (the first Teen Challenge home for women) in Garrison, New York. After spending 17 months there, I graduated the program.

God changed my life into something I never thought it could be. It was there that I learned that I was smart and had gifts that God wanted me to develop. The director of the program recruited me to work in the office doing various jobs. At first I didn't know why she chose me. Then at some point I realized that she saw something in me that I hadn't seen in myself. It was her belief in me that first instilled the confidence to help me excel in other areas. She gave me hope and I don't think she ever realized how much that affected me.

A couple of years later I married my husband. When we began our relationship he was a Bible school student and I told him that I never wanted to be a pastor's wife. He thought that was fine, because he didn't want to be a pastor. Apparently, God had different plans. He finished Bible school, and at his graduation party was hired as a pastor in the very church I grew up in. Over the years, we had three children and were sent out to plant a church. Then, after a long difficult court battle, God intervened and I regained custody of my oldest daughter. I often struggled as a stay-at-home mom. I battled depression and was very overwhelmed with the everyday tasks of caring for small, rambunctious children. It was a miracle I made it through those years and the fact that I did is only

another testimony of God's grace in my life.

As the children grew older, I felt that it was time to plan for my future. I knew one day my kids would have their own lives and if I didn't have something to occupy my time I would probably fall into depression or spend my time meddling in their lives. That's when I decided to do something that I had been so afraid to do; I had never even considered it. I decided to go back to school and become a nurse. I felt that this was a calling that God had placed on my life and I was finally ready to tackle it.

As part of the process of enrolling in school, I met with the dean of nursing to discuss my sordid past. She cautioned me in taking the nursing track because she felt that dealing with the distribution of controlled substances could put my sobriety in jeopardy. I listened to her concerns, but I knew that this was what I was called to do. She then explained that although she had concerns, there was nothing any one could do to stop me from finishing school and she didn't believe that my past would prevent me from obtaining a nursing license.

I struggled my way through nursing school, wanting to give up at every turn. Eventually, after years of juggling difficult school work while raising four children and being the wife of a senior pastor, I graduated from nursing school with honors. The Bible states in Luke 1:37 "For with God, nothing is impossible." I now truly have a changed life.

After I finished sharing my story, I asked the young girl standing alongside the highway if there was anything I could do to help her get clean. I told her about our church, the 12-step programs I have been affiliated with, and mentioned the local Teen Challenge, just seconds down the road. Then I gave her my phone number and a five dollar bill to get something to eat. Some of you may disagree with that action, but I felt I owed her for her time. Her eyes lit up when I told her I would pray for her and she stated that I had, in fact, given her hope and that she would call me. Driving away I noticed a song playing on my radio, a version of "Amazing Grace (My Chains Fell Off)" the lyrics being, "I was once was lost, but now I'm found, I was blind, but now I see. My chains are gone. I've been set free. My God, my Savior has ransomed me." I knew I had made a difference.

A week or two after I met that young girl on the side of the road I received a text message from her. She thanked me for pulling over and sharing my story with her. She had entered a sober house, had been clean for a little over a week and wanted to get together with me. I don't know what the future holds for her, but I'm excited to watch her story be written. Sometimes, all someone needs is a little bit of hope.

Chapter 6
From Pain to Purpose

Todd Sheehan

Growing up in southern New Hampshire wasn't horrible by any stretch of the imagination. My life as a child was very normal, with loving parents, siblings and lots of friends to experience the joys of life with. My childhood was filled with wonderful Christmas holidays, family vacations and years dedicated to sports. It wasn't until I was 16 years old that I smoked pot for the first time. This was the gateway drug for me as it made me feel good and quickly escalated to me experimenting with different drugs. From there, it was a steady descent for me into the world of addiction. I was trying to fill a void inside that could never be satisfied.

"There is a way that seems right to a man,
but its end is the way of death."
Proverbs 14:12 (NKJV)

The beginning of the end came for me on, Oct 20, 2003. Death was made very real to me, as I held my lifeless girlfriend; dead from a drug overdose. One of the last things we discussed was that this can't be all that life has to offer and there must be something better for us. We wanted to change our lives, and we decided that tomorrow would be a good time to start. We decided that tomorrow we would make a change. Tomorrow we would seek help. Tomorrow we would face our demons. The tragic reality of my situation, and one of the great tragedies of life, is that we put things off until tomorrow, and sometimes tomorrow never comes. Sometimes we don't get a second chance.

After her death, the hole inside of me grew deeper. The void that I was trying to fill became more intense. The only way that I knew how to deal with the pain was to get high.

> My strength came from a bag of dope;
> my faith was in a bottle of pills.

As a drug addict, I was spiritually dead, I was trying to fill a void, take away my pain and run from my hopeless circumstances.

Two months had passed since the tragic loss of my girlfriend and my life hit rock bottom. That spot on the floor where I held her lifeless body was filled with pain and grief and the question of why it was her life taken and not mine. I did not understand why she had to die. Desperate, I simply asked for the intervention of a Heavenly Father. Out of options and at the end of myself, I asked God to change the direction of my life.

"I will answer them before they even call to me. While they are still talking about their needs, I will go ahead and answer their prayers."
Isaiah 65:24 (TLB)

God answers prayer! I woke up to the phone ringing. It was my mother telling me to "take a look at the Manchester edition of the Union Leader" (The local newspaper). There was an article on Teen Challenge and the brand new facility that had opened its doors in Manchester, New Hampshire. As I read the article over and over again, I felt a small glimmer of hope; I felt a light shining on my dark circumstances. I knew that afternoon, after mustering up the courage to call Teen Challenge to find out what needed to be done to gain admission, that this was where I needed to be. God had opened the door of hope in my life.

"For I am about to do something new. See, I have already begun! Do you not see it? I will make a pathway through the wilderness. I will create rivers in the dry wasteland."
Isaiah 43:19 (NLT)

For five days, my home was the detox floor at the Catholic Medical Center in Manchester, New Hampshire. It was the first step in the admissions process. With all the toxins that a lifestyle of addiction brings, it takes a long time to have a clear head, but I was taking it day by day, excited about entering Teen Challenge! At 9AM on January 15, 2004, I left the detox at the hospital and made the short journey from the west side of the city, over to the east side of the city. Arriving at Teen Challenge broken, lost, and filled with pain, I was putting my faith in God for the first time.

"May the God of hope fill you with all joy and peace as you trust him, so that you may overflow with hope by the power of the Holy Spirit."
Romans 15:13

Getting out of the car and walking up to the front door of the program is a moment I will never forget. As I approached the top step, the door swung open suddenly and out came a student in the program with a big smile on his face saying "Welcome to Teen Challenge!" I was shocked and caught off guard as this individual had just entered the program only 30 days before. I knew I was entering a drug rehabilitation program and didn't understand how he could possibly be so happy. He seemed to have this indescribable joy and contentment! I stood there on that doorstep reflecting on where my life was, thinking about my failures, and not knowing what the future was going to hold. But at that moment, one thing was clear, one thing was certain; I wanted to be able to smile the way he smiled. I wanted the joy he had in his life, in my life. I wanted the contentment and happiness that was on display as he welcomed me to my new home.

"Therefore, if anyone is in Christ, he is a new creation;
old things have passed away;
behold, all things have become new."
2 Corinthians 5:17 (NKJV)

Teen Challenge is a place of change and over the next fifteen months I would have to look and deal with, the man in the mirror. No longer running from emotions or feelings of the past, but allowing God's Word, and the power of the Holy Spirit to change me into a new creation! I had to set aside who I was, for the sake of who God wanted me to become. I had to set aside what I wanted to do, for the sake of what God wanted to do with my life.

I accepted Christ as my Lord and Savior
shortly after entering the program and
my life has not been the same since.

My faith is no longer in a bag of dope or a bottle of pills, my faith is in God and my strength comes through a personal relationship with him.

"The God who gives life to the dead and calls things
that are not as though they were."
Romans 4:17b (NLT)

God has taken the pain of that horrible night and turned it into a purpose, to be a part of the solution instead of the problem. I completed the program on April 29, 2005. God has given me a passion to live and to reach out to the lost, hopeless drug addicts. I daily feel the presence of my girlfriend giving me the courage and the strength to move forward on this journey of faith, saying "Never give up, never give up!"

"Now to him who is able to do immeasurably more than we
ask or imagine, according to his power that is
at work within us."
Ephesians 3:20

Eleven years ago I was unsure if I would be able to remain out of prison, or free from addiction to pills and heroin, and if you would have told me what God had planned, I would not have believed you. Since that date with destiny on the doorstep of Teen Challenge New Hampshire in 2004, God has been faithful! God saved me, changed me and set this captive free!

On September 16, 2006, I married the girl of my dreams! Samantha also grew up in New Hampshire and has a deep appreciation for the Teen Challenge ministry. Her father Steve started the center in Manchester and Samantha often traveled and promoted the ministry in churches all over New England. She has a heart for broken humanity and seeing lives restored from the horrors of addiction.

"This is my command - be strong and courageous!
Do not be afraid or discouraged.
For the Lord your God is with you wherever you go."
Joshua 1:9 (NLT)

Samantha and I were quite comfortable with our situation in New Hampshire and I was not looking for another ministry opportunity. I was working for Teen Challenge on their program development team, helping to organize fundraising opportunities and traveling to churches around the state promoting the ministry and the life changing message of Christ. Samantha had a great job at a medical office. We were living in a nice house with a fenced in yard and a pool, enjoying our family being close by.

Then things changed drastically and quickly! We would soon move to Newark, New Jersey, where we were called to and given the amazing opportunity to serve as directors for Teen Challenge, New Jersey. The center was located in the heart of Newark, in an area filled with gang activity, drug deals, gunshots and many broken and hopeless lives. This was a great contrast from the scenery in southern New Hampshire. To make matters worse, we are dedicated, and loyal Boston sports fans, so North Jersey was not what we were looking for.

Then the Teen Challenge program in Jersey was only weeks away from closing its doors. After many funding issues and leadership transitions, this was going to be a mission and assignment that would take years of dedication and hard work to see Teen Challenge New Jersey be what God want it to be; a place that changes lives.

We spent five years in Newark, rebuilding the program, developing the leadership team, building relationships in the state, seeing the population of the center grow from five men in the program when we arrived, to thirty men living in 4,100 square feet of living space. It was clear that we had outgrown our facility and desperately needed something larger that would accommodate our ministry needs.

> "Jesus replied,
> "What is impossible with man is possible with God."
> Luke 18:27

What happened next still amazes me now as I reflect

on the faithfulness of God. He only requires us to say "yes" and follow His lead. He desires us to be faithful with what we have and to trust Him for everything else.

Then the call came. My friend George Costa called me about a potential property. George was a board member for a youth camp in north central New Jersey. The camp had been a thriving ministry for years, bringing inner city kids to a location with trees, fresh air, swimming and most importantly the gospel message and an opportunity to encounter Christ. As years passed, vision, funding, resources and man power would diminish and the camp that was once flourishing with Kingdom work.

I met George at the property and was immediately amazed, 88 acres of land in Hunterdon County with more than 20 buildings including, a dining hall, chapel, administration building, dorms, garages, and sheds. This would be a place where Teen Challenge New Jersey would have the potential to provide a better environment for our students and an opportunity to grow. The facilities were in a state of disrepair and I looked at George and jokingly said, "There is hundreds of thousands of dollars of repair and renovation work to be done, the only way this property would work for us is if you gave it to us!" George looked at me very seriously and said, "That's what we would like to do."

This was the miracle we were waiting for, and on August 31, 2014, the property was ours. We immediately started renovating four buildings that would accommodate our current ministry needs and allow us to relocate from our Newark facility. On December 31, 2014, we moved out of our inner city Newark location to our amazing new campus: a place that will allow us to grow and see the nets of the Kingdom drastically expanded here in New Jersey.

"Therefore, my dear brothers, stand firm. Let nothing move you. Always give yourself fully to the work of the Lord, because you know that your labor in the Lord is not in vain."
1 Corinthians 15:58

God has expanded not only our ministry, but my family as well. Evangeline Frances Sheehan was born on May 25, 2013; we just celebrated her second birthday. She is the joy of our lives. Samantha currently works in our administration department and we make our home in Hunterdon County, New Jersey. After completing my studies with Global University, I am a credentialed minister with the New Jersey District of the Assemblies of God. My life mission is to see more lives changed and families restored by the power of Christ in New Jersey! I believe my pain has been long gone but it provided the path for me to find purpose. What Jesus has done for me, He will do for you. **"The best is yet to come!"**

Chapter 7
Atheist, Altar, Accomplished

Jonathan Mello

It was a warm summer morning in late June. As the sun rose, the light reflected off of the dew that hung from blades of grass in the fields, the manner of which can only be described as angelic. There was something different about this day; time almost seemed to be slowing down as the anticipation was building. It was a day foretold in ancient writings, a day where legends would be forged. It was the day that Jonathan Christopher Mello was born.... well it wasn't that magical.

Growing up my childhood was great. I was born in Washington D.C, and grew up in a small town on Cape Cod, Massachusetts. I was raised in a very nurturing home, my mom and dad wanted the best life that my sister and I could have and it showed. There was never a time when there was something I wanted, but couldn't have. I still joke with my mom occasionally about the guitar I had to have so I could be like

Santana, but it only lasted through one practice (my niece is now using it for her lessons so it didn't go to waste). My mom imparted a great sense of pride in our culture and family values that I still carry to this day. I was raised to treat my elders with the respect they deserved, with the understanding that respect was something that had to be earned. We were close, rarely were meals eaten away from the kitchen table, we enjoyed each other's company. My home was a safe place and as I reflect, while there were "issues" taking place, my mom really sheltered me from it all.

After my dad had been involved in a serious car accident things started to shift. (Read Chris Mello's story in Chapter 4) We had moved to New Bedford, Massachusetts and he was no longer living with us. I remember being unclear of the circumstances, frustrated even, that I was now in a new place with new people. Sure I had visited there before, most of my family was from New Bedford, but I never really interacted socially with the kids my age that weren't related to me. I remember the overwhelming feeling that I just didn't fit in. Even worse I was beginning to experience rejection, something I'd never had to deal with before, and I felt the one person that should have been there wasn't, my dad. I couldn't really process the range of emotions; the lack of clarity surrounding why life had so dramatically changed, only complicated the matter. I blamed my mom as if she was the problem, I didn't know any better, I just knew I didn't feel as safe as I once did.

It wasn't all that bad, a lot was good. My dad was always financially supportive and my mom worked hard to make sure we had everything we needed and more. I had so many older cousins and it felt great to be close to family now. But a year later, when I got into junior high school things became worse. Not only did I not fit in, but now it was manifested with aggression. Sports, video games and comics were my outlets as I looked for opportunities to be someone else.

Growing up I was exposed to Christian principles and biblical practices, but none of it ever took any serious root.

Going through all those emotions I couldn't really comprehend the idea of a "loving God" who was in control. It simply didn't fit my worldview or my perceived reality. During a seventh grade biology class the "Theory of Evolution" was taught. "That's it!" I thought, now everything made sense. There was no God; I made a decision moving forward to grab hold of an atheistic worldview. I challenged everything I thought: What's right? What's wrong? With no God surely there can be no real consequences. God became nothing more a fictional character used by parents to keep us in check. I remember coming home one day shortly after my insight and telling my mom, who had invoked God into the conversation, "Ha! There is no God." She said, "You just have to have faith." To which I responded, "What is faith? Define it!" To which she replied, "Faith is not something you see, it's what you believe in your heart." I would devote quite a bit of time throughout these years studying all things that lent credibility to this belief. My problem wasn't with Jesus, Buddha or Mohammad. Rather with the very idea, the very notion that there was a God. Some benevolent being that actually cared about our reality. To me he was nothing more than a crutch for people who couldn't cope, and I had no need for that.

The next year, I met a girl who would get alcohol from her parent's cabinet and bring it to me after school. My mom was working nights so we would all just hang out at my house. I loved the way it made me feel, I felt confident again. I began to realize the more stupid stuff I did, the more accepted I was by my peers, the crazier, the better. I cast off and continued to ignore any sense of morality that I had, and just became numb to it. My best friend's mom forbade him to spend time with me any more because I had become a terrible influence. By the time high school rolled around, I was smoking marijuana constantly and pretty much quit all the sports I was involved in. My grades were still good though and I spent the following two summers in college prep programs. That became the great balancing act, trying to keep my feet in two worlds. On one hand I was sure I'd end up in college somewhere, on the other I rapidly started getting into all kinds of trouble with the law. My new group of friends had already dropped out of school. I began to hustle for pocket change and commit robberies to keep up with the lifestyle I saw portrayed and so desperately wanted. The repercussions led to me dropping out of high school, DSS (Department of Children and Families) custody, and a couple detentions in DYS (Department of Youth Services) facilities.

Due to some legal issues, I left New Bedford, Massachusetts when I was 17; I had to get out of there. I moved back to Cape Cod, Massachusetts with a plan to go back to school and go to a community college, and work my way up from there. I got a job at a restaurant and soon found I had little motivation to do anything but earn enough money to keep up with the perpetual party lifestyle I now lived. As soon as I got off from work I went to a bar or a local party. As long as I could still pull off a 16 hour shift the next day I felt everything was under control.

This would go on for a few years and while I had always thought New Bedford was the issue, I quickly realized trouble seemed to follow me wherever I went. Simply put, I was the problem.

I continued to find myself in legal trouble from new arrests to probation violations.

It came to a head when I received a charge that carried a significant mandatory sentence. I pleaded out to reduce the charges, but it violated another probation order. This left me in the precarious position of having to walk a straight line for the next year. Four months later, I violated the terms by picking up a new charge, and as a result I spent the next few months at the Ash Street Jail & Regional Lock-Up in New Bedford, Massachusetts and the Bristol County House of Correction in Dartmouth, Massachusetts. While at Ash Street awaiting the sentence, unaware of how much time I would end up serving, I came to a stark realization. I thought to myself: "This is it Jonathan, this is your life." This was when I grasped the reality that there were no longer two worlds to choose from anymore, no more options. I had blown every opportunity, and the saddest thing about this sudden perception was that I was all right with it. I no longer had to try and walk the line that I had obviously failed miserably at. I was finally content with who I was, the conflict was gone.

Days after coming to this realization, I received a letter in the mail. My first thought was, "I never get mail here." The letter was from my dad and it opened with this line: "God has a plan for your life; I know you don't believe this, but God has a plan for your life." He went on to write about what he was doing and the program he was now involved in, Teen Challenge in Brockton, Massachusetts. He then wrote out the testimony of how his life had changed. Honestly, I didn't get much more from the letter than thinking that, at least my dad got his life together. I had time on my hands so I thought "What harm could it do?" I went to the library and grabbed a Bible and *The Acts of King Arthur and His Noble Knights* by John Steinbeck. I opened the Bible and started reading. I made it all the way to Genesis 1:28 before closing it in disgust and tossing it aside. I thought this has to be the stupidest thing ever, what happened to the dinosaurs! How can anyone believe this nonsense? Then I proceeded to read the other book I had grabbed.

A few months after I was released, I found myself in violation of my parole again. I went to plead with my probation officer and he flat out told me he would be asking that I serve the full term of my suspended sentence. I went out and hired a lawyer to try and get the time reduced as much as possible. I was fortunate, or so I thought, that the lawyer I hired happened to be old classmate of my probation officer. The probation officer ended up sounding more like my attorney. The judge looked at me as he thumbed through my rap sheet and bellowed, "Mr. Mello, I lock people up for less than this. If you come before me again you will serve the full remainder of the suspended sentence. I don't care who's in here." My lawyer said to me walking out of the courtroom as I thanked him, "Jonathan if you violate again, don't waste your money on me." A week later I was arrested on a new charge.

After skipping my hearings, my dad called me and said, “Hey, I heard you got arrested again, what are you going to do?” I told him I’d go on the run for the summer and in the fall turn myself in. He said to me “Why don’t you come to Teen Challenge? That there might even be a way for him to defer my sentence to the program.” My objections were obvious, but he said I didn’t really have to believe anything, I just had to go along with the program. I figured I had nothing to lose and I might as well give it a shot. After all, I was sure I could find a way to weasel out of this situation like so many others.

On July 5, 2001 I entered the doors of Teen Challenge. I was 20 years old. The only thing I hoped for was to avoid a lengthy sentence. After a few days I was convinced everyone there had lost their minds. I would actively engage in conversation with anyone who tried to persuade me to their faith, but otherwise I was left well enough alone. I mean if it was working for them, why mess up a good thing?

> One night I was engaged in a friendly conversation over the existence of God with my roommate.

He said to me, “Jonathan it’s late and I don’t know what else to tell you. All I know is that if you ask God to reveal himself to you, He will.” I thought, what could I say to that but goodnight?

A few days later we were all in a chapel service; I was seated in the back row. I didn't participate in worship and I couldn't tell you who or what was preached, I was completely disengaged. However, I vividly remember the altar call. There were about 17 men on the campus and I had become familiar with their stories. The years of addiction that was represented here simply could not be ignored. Most of them, at this point, were surrounding the platform sobbing and crying out to this God. I paused to observe what was going on. "This wasn't the normal behavior of an addict," I thought. I began to attempt to rationalize what was taking place, trying to make sense of it all. As I was searching for some sort of justification, the thought hit me and the words came out of my mouth. "Yeah right, God, if you're real, reveal yourself," I proclaimed with such arrogance. Right then I was urged to pick up the Bible that I was made to carry around. I glanced over at it and brushed the thought off for a few minutes before reaching over and grabbing it. Lifting it up, it fell open; I didn't turn any pages and my eyes darted to a passage. "The Lord has done what He planned; He has fulfilled his word, which He decreed long ago. He has overthrown you without pity, He has let the enemy gloat over you, He has exalted the horn of your foes." (Lamentations. 2:17)

Words can never fully capture what took place next, all I know for sure is, it wasn't something I was searching for. I immediately thought back to the letter my father had written, and began to be saturated by the overwhelming feeling that He, God, was there through it all. During this epiphany, my mind raced to three occasions I managed to walk away from unharmed. At the time I simply thought I was bullet proof. It was an immediate shift from thinking it was my good fortune that got me through, to seeing that it was God's hand that guided and protected me to this very moment; "The Lord has done what He has planned." In the book of Ezekiel there is a prophecy where God declares that he will remove the heart of stone and replace it with a heart of flesh (Ezekiel 11:19-20). I had learned to suppress emotions; lower my standards and morals throughout the years, I had become numb to it all. It was as if all of my morals, beliefs and values that I had growing up were immediately restored to their former state. As I began to ponder the mess I had made of my life the feeling of guilt that was rapidly building upon my shoulders, was devastating me. I didn't know what to do, so I stood up and walked up to the altar. Sobbing, looking for relief to the burden I was now carrying, I cried out to Jesus to save me. I didn't fully understand what I was doing, or what I was getting myself into for that matter. I just knew there was something about Jesus that could bring me relief. It was then that He saved me.

Everything changed moving forward, I had a new outlook and a new perspective on life. I began the "heavy lifting" of change and I'm forever grateful to Teen Challenge for being there to help me along in the process. I knew I had to change; I had to rewire and rethink just about everything I was prone to do. I didn't just learn about God but I also learned how to apply his Word to my life. I learned life skills necessary to help me cope and overcome the enormous issues I had developed with anger, forgiveness and love. It taught me discipline and how to take responsibility for my actions rather than look for excuses. I was surrounded by a variety of pastors and mentors that continually and sacrificially assisted and guided me in my development as a Christian. Through this process I wasn't sure where it was going to take me but I wanted to find out. Best of all I got to do it with my dad.

> For the first time in a long time I had hope again.
> I knew my life was going to be different.

Sure I struggled with difficult habits and behaviors that I had established over the years, but I knew I wasn't alone in it. I knew that despite the obstacle, whatever it was, I could move past it. God was truly bigger than it all.

After I graduated, I decided to stay on with Teen Challenge for an internship, and then to seek employment there. I had the opportunity to give back and help others along the way in their journey as those who had done so for me. I felt a strong calling to the ministry and began my studies. I was credentialed and received my license to preach from the Assemblies of God in 2004. I received a Diploma in Urban Ministry in 2014 and I am currently working on a Masters of Divinity from Gordon-Conwell Theological Seminary. I continue to solidify my foundation in ministry to better serve Him. Throughout the last 14 years I've worked at several Teen Challenge campuses in the New England area. I currently serve as the Associate Director of the Boston campus, the same center that I went through and graduated from. To me there is no greater reward than to see someone come in broken and lost and then find their way. I've seen countless men and women become radically changed and leave here with hope; fathers, mothers, sons and daughters restored. It's evidence that God is still doing GREAT WORKS today.

This journey has been an amazing one. My relationship with my mom has never been better and she got her son back. I've been able to work in the same organization with my dad and our bond has never been stronger. I'm able to be a brother, uncle and a role model to my sister and my two beautiful nieces. I met my amazingly, wonderful wife Tabatha whom I married in 2006. (Read Tabatha's story in Changed Lives Book 1) After almost a decade of marriage I've learned what commitment really means. I'm blessed to be able to share my life with her. We also share a house with our two dogs, Spurgeon and Buster. I feel like this journey is still getting started, and I'm excited for whatever may come next. He saved me and I'm humbled by the thought that I truly deserve none of this. I couldn't ask for anything more.

Chapter 8
From Darkness to Light

Brian Dube

"Once in a while you get shown the light, in the strangest of places if you look at it right."
- Scarlet Begonias, The Grateful Dead

"The Light shines in the darkness, and the darkness did not comprehend it."
- John 1:5 (NASB)

Addiction can happen to anyone—as can grace. Believe me.

I grew up in a safe, comfortable, quiet New England town. My parents were hardworking people who loved me a great deal, as did my younger sister. There was no tragedy, no abuse. My home life was stable and I always felt unconditional love. My aunts and uncles lived nearby and we spent a lot of time with our extended family. There were cookouts in the summer and holidays were always spent visiting family and friends. I lacked for nothing. It was as close to Eden as childhood gets.

Right down to the creeping presence of darkness.

Hell, wrote Sartre, is other people, and that's pretty much how I felt as a child. I was a friendly kid, eager to love and be loved, but fidgety and anxious, so I had a lot of trouble making friends. I was extremely sensitive. I'd think and worry about things more than most kids my age, taking the cruelties of childhood very hard, which made me especially fun to tease. Whatever nervousness or anxiety I had became worse as I so desperately tried to fit in. But no matter what I tried, I couldn't make close friends. Instead, I was often made fun of. One time, I was unexpectedly invited to play outside with the neighborhood kids. I ran out, delighted to finally be part of the crowd, only to find out they had written horrible things about me in chalk on the street. They'd only invited me outside so they could laugh at me. The pain was--excruciating. Unable to make friends with kids my age, I spent Friday nights eating fish and chips with my dad. Try as I could, I could not connect with other people, or with God.

My family was like most, I guess, when it came to God--lukewarm overall. This wasn't enough, despite their best intentions, to keep my darkness at bay. My mother believed in God, my dad did not (though I would not find this out until years later). So we rarely attended church. The only real talk of God was at my parochial school. I made my confirmation in eighth grade, but I had no idea what it meant. I just remember being asked to "reject Satan and all his works," which made sense to me. I was taught some basics about God and the Bible but, being inquisitive, had more questions than they had answers, which were mostly, "You must simply have faith." For me, that wasn't good enough. Not even close. What kind of God would permit the vicious bullying I endured, and the other cruelties in the world? No answers came. So I began to doubt the very existence of a loving God, doubts that only worsened in my big city high school.

When I left my small parochial school for high school, I encountered a whole new level of bullying. There were lots of fights and as a small town, nervous kid, I was often a target. Once, a kid picked me up over his shoulders while another ran toward us and knocked me backwards onto the hard school floor.

> Lying on the ground in pain, trying to catch my breath, I looked up to see dozens of kids in the hall, laughing.

It took all my strength to not cry and most days that's

how I felt. I was anxious, afraid and searching for answers with none in sight. All I could think about was why am I here? Is there a God? What is the meaning of it all? Why are people so cruel to each other? Sometimes, when I was around friendly people, I thought maybe God was real. But most often, God seemed distant and silent. As if He wasn't there at all.

With all this pain and confusion, I began to consider myself an Atheist. The world seemed dark and desolate. People were almost never decent. Faith, to me, seemed like wishful thinking. My family, though wonderful, were simply naïve. I loved them dearly, but couldn't relate to their "white picket fence" world. In fact, I wanted none of it. To me, it was just wishful thinking. What kind of God would sit by and allow the injustice I saw everywhere in the world? I saw only the terrible things people do to each other. And darkness began to take hold.

Instead of seeking guidance from God, I sought it in tragic stories, tragic heroes, tragic songs, the dire, heartbreaking and the bleak. I loved the dark, nihilistic writings of Hunter S. Thompson and Hemingway and the wild, outlaw adventures of Jack Kerouac and Ken Kesey. The imaginative and limitless world of the music of the Grateful Dead provided a welcome, temporary escape, but it seemed the only true things were, as Jim Morrison put it, that no one here gets out alive and your only friend is the end. Convinced of this,

I set about creating a deliberately tragic life for myself. I became restless, detached and arrogant. Since there is no God, I thought, the best we can do is increase pleasure and minimize pain. I was simply living for the moment and life became a joke and everything in it a target for my humor. Not only did the humor provide a welcome defense but this cynical attitude made me popular! If they were laughing at your jokes then at least, for the moment, you seemed to fit in. Maybe, just maybe, they didn't hate you.

Before long, the careless, flippant attitude that won me laughter and applause from the crowd turned into utter disrespect for all authority. I became defiant toward everyone. When my teachers told me I could improve my grades if I applied myself, I would just smile and blow them off. To me it seemed pointless. Why bother? In a world without God, it's not about grades but fun in the moment. Thoughts of the future only brought frustration and worry so I didn't think about it. My parents never stopped loving me unconditionally, but to a jaded high school junior, it was a lot more fun to be out with friends, so I blew off my Friday fish dinners with my dad. Dad's been gone for over seven years now and I'd give anything for one more dinner with him. But back then? Life was a non-stop party and I had no time for hanging around with my parents or looking for a nonexistent God.

Once I got my license, I was almost never home. I'd

finally become part of the crowd I'd so desperately tried to fit in with, and that's where I wanted to be. By my senior year, skipping school, partying, chasing girls and doing drugs with these new friends was my way of life.

Then there was drinking. I'll never forget the first time I got drunk. Rather than feel sick and regret it, I fell in love. To me, there was no better feeling. I was no longer self-conscious and all my inhibition went away. In fact, I became the life of the party. I'd do anything for a laugh. I'd eat anything, drink anything, steal things, start fights with people, make lewd comments to girls and do pretty much anything for attention. Excess drinking became an all-purpose problem solver, and I was elated to put my life under its control.

Alcohol and cigarettes led quickly to marijuana. Before long I was overdoing that too. I mean, really overdoing it. Some friends sat me down and said they were afraid for me. I drank way too much, they said, and the drugs were changing me. I'd become distant, cold and rather unpleasant. In my arrogance, I laughed them off. To me, straight people like them just existed, going through motions but I wanted more and more. Excess soon became something I would be known for. I'd challenge people to see who could drink more shots of Jack Daniels. No one ever beat me. Back then, that won me applause. Finally, I thought I was well liked, when in fact, I was simply the night's entertainment. Others tried to help me, but

I had it all figured out. Yes, I was going to hell in a bucket, as Bob Weir put it. But at least I was enjoying the ride.

Far from heeding the constant warnings and advice from those who loved me, I dove headfirst with my buddies into the bad choices that shaped and defined the next 15 years of my life. We were a bunch of kids simply looking to make life more enjoyable, living by our own set of rules, and there weren't many. If it felt good, we did it and for a while it seemed to be working fine. In reality, the consequences were already piling up, though it took me a long time to see them.

Sad to say, I was not a good influence on my sister or anyone else around me. It was quite the opposite. I was the one who'd encourage people to drink more, try new drugs, stay out later and tell lies to their parents. Sadly, there were many kids who used their first drug with me. I manipulated people into getting me whatever I wanted regardless of the effects on them. Like Tom Sawyer, I'd convince them I was actually doing them a favor--and I believed it! I'd convince people to call in sick to work or skip classes simply because I didn't want the party to end, ever.

> People would crash at my house almost every night, blowing off responsibilities and relationships, all because I never wanted to be left alone with my thoughts.

I would do and take anything to avoid the nagging feelings of emptiness, keeping myself sufficiently distracted so I had no awareness of the other lives I was helping ruin.

I had turned my back completely on God, and treated everyone around me with indifference. I was too deep into the darkness to care. Though I had forgotten about God, and His love, He hadn't forgotten me. Into my dark, hopeless life crept the most amazing light I'd ever seen, a true gift from God, though it took me a long time to comprehend it. It was the woman who'd one day save my life, my future wife, Rebecca.

Towards the end of my senior year of high school, I met Bek, and everything started to change. She was a Christian but I didn't know what that meant, and didn't care. All I knew was she was fun and gorgeous and sweet, and that's all that mattered--at first. But as I got to know her, I realized I didn't know anyone my age like her. She was selfless and kind and helpful, a very positive person. She'd encourage me to make better choices without making me feel like a loser. She'd come to my house when I would still be sleeping at one pm and with a big smile, open the blinds letting the light pour in. To me, that's what she was: light. I was struck by how incredibly mature she was. She seemed to exist above all the nonsense that made up those years. While most of us were busy with superficial pursuits and criticizing one another, she never took part. I felt she was a much better person than me, and I began to want to be like her, and to believe that was possible, because she believed it. She gave me hope. I fell deeply, forever in love with her. I realize now that by sending her and others like her to me, God, on whom I'd turned my back, was turning His face to me.

But I wasn't ready to let my party life go, and turn my face to God. Instead, I separated myself into two lives, one light, and one dark. I'd party with my friends and take on my "Animal House" persona on the weekends but when I was with my new girlfriend during the week, I was . . . different. In short, I tried to serve two masters--with predictable results.

A few months after meeting Rebecca, I graduated high school (barely), and began to attend a local community college off and on. My pattern of heavy drug use continued, as did my lack of interest and effort in anything but partying. My friend's dad owned a bar and we had the keys. Needless to say, this increased our appetite for partying and the arrogant attitude that we were different. We knew all the right people and had all the right connections to easily get us out of any trouble. This undeserved entitlement enabled me to roar down a path of destruction that hurt not just me, but everyone who loved me. I'd spend every paycheck at the bar and on cigarettes and drugs. Why think about the future? Live for today! Never planning, never stopping to look around, life became a blur of meaningless work, erratically attended classes, hardcore partying and trying to slow down a little to spend time with this girl who represented the hope of a better life.

On occasion, I felt guilty. I cared little for myself, but began to see the pain I was causing those who loved me. Slowly but surely, light was creeping in. But when it did--when those guilty thoughts and feelings grew--I did what addicts always do. I found a way to rationalize and justify my drug use. Hey, I was in school and worked with mentally challenged adults. I had a nice girl that I had decided to be faithful to. I was a hero! (That's right, my hero was . . . me.) Yes, I was a selfish addict who cared little for anyone else, but I never cheated on my girlfriend. I was a terrific guy!

It's funny the warped morality that exists in our lives during those times. I thought I didn't really have a drug issue because all I did regularly was smoke marijuana. The other drugs I did occasionally--cocaine, mescaline, LSD--I could take or leave. Then there were months that I didn't use drugs at all. Yes, in those months, I drank heavily. But . . . You get the picture. I was simply deceiving myself, or trying to, into believing that my dark, ugly, destructive life was actually something pure and bright. The reality? From the age of 17 until I was 33, I never went longer than 30 days without some drug or drink. And my addiction harmed everyone I touched. But in my head, like I said, I was a hero—until the ugly consequences began piling up too high to ignore.

To start with, I was miserable. My "If it feels good, do it" plan was a big failure because, before long, nothing felt good. I felt alone and utterly unfulfilled by anything that I thought should fill me. The only spark of brightness was Rebecca. I began stepping deeper into that other world—the world of hope, and light. I began trying harder to do the right thing. I wasn't sure how or what that was, I just knew that when I was with Bek, I was happy and I was hopeful. I wanted to become more and more like that. But, as with everything I'd done by that point, I was going to do it on my terms. I was still convinced that I, and only I, was in control of my universe. Not God. Not drugs. Me.

I decided moderation was the key. If I did well during the week--made good money, avoided drinking and drugs, hung out with my girlfriend and was faithful--I not only could, but deserved to spend the weekends as a blackout drunk. Again with my warped morality, but it seemed like a great way of life, pursued by many people I knew. (Talk about the blind leading the blind!)

The reality was moderation was simply never a concept I was able to adopt. I was, from the very beginning, prone to excess and to self-destruction. Once, when I was talking about the need to take better care of myself, Rebecca remarked, "You have been slowly killing yourself since the day I met you. You just change the method from time to time."

The long and short of it is, ANY plan to control your universe that involves you (or anything other than God) at the helm is headed for colossal failure. Believe me, I've tried them all. Wealth. Prestige. Popularity. Hedonism. Intellectualism. Even the white picket fence...

After a few years, Bek and I got married. We had kids. I got into computers and got a good job making great money. I belonged to a church and we served the youth. I believed it likely that God existed, but refused to give Him control of anything in my life. I still wanted to do it my way. I slowed down the partying and hardly ever drank, but when I did I'd fall right back into the same old habits. I'd chain smoke cigarettes, use marijuana or whatever else presented itself, get blackout drunk, and wake up the next day to an upset wife, empty wallet and a bunch of regrets--and still, the nagging emptiness, that nothing was able to take away.

Why was the void still there? Nothing seemed to lift my darkness. I could be in a crowded room surrounded by friends and still feel all alone.

> My years living on the edge had left me hollow and cold to the bone.

I was king of my world, making all my own decisions, and every one of them left me empty. Lost in darkness. Meanwhile, my life continued to rot. I began to have health problems, money problems, marital problems, work problems, all of which I managed to keep just barely under control. And so it went, until somewhere in the fog of drinking, marijuana use and a generally underachieving and mediocre existence, I was introduced to Oxycontin—and hell on earth.

It started out innocently enough. These things always do. I was given the drug for migraine headaches. I told my doctor nothing of my history with drugs and alcohol. At first, Oxy was a miracle. Finally, I had a warm, cottony cushion against the pain and the darkness of life. Almost immediately I began to abuse the drug. I took more than I was supposed to and within two years was taking almost ten times the dose I had been prescribed daily. Within three years I was crushing up the pills and snorting them. Within four, I was stealing and lying to buy them off of the street.

My doctors always caught on to my addiction and cut me off, but I always found someone somewhere to get me my drugs. My life revolved around coming up with about $500 every day. I would then desperately call drug dealers to meet me in different neighborhoods that I had lived not far from my whole life, but for good reason had never been to. Every bit of control I had, whether real or perceived, was disappearing. I was hopelessly enslaved. The power of this drug was unimaginable to me and it simply overtook me. If there is a tool of the devil more powerful than addiction, I don't know what it is. All my control was gone, and it wasn't God I had invited into that space. Darkness had overtaken me.

Before I knew it, five blurry years had passed. I'd now been to detox four times, had spent over $100,000 and had lost a very good job. Everything I thought would never happen did. I overdosed in front of my wife and kids and ended up hospitalized. My life caused the people I cared most about so much grief. I was not the husband nor the father my wife and my kids deserved. Those who loved me felt powerless to help me. I loved them all and was physically present in their lives, but I was emotionally and spiritually empty. I was living in chaos and confusion and things were getting darker each day.

There wasn't much left of me to surrender when my family finally called Teen Challenge. I certainly did not know it then, but God in His grace had a plan and it was a plan only He could carry out. I was brought to Teen Challenge Brockton in March of 2007 and to say my life has not been the same since is an understatement. When I entered Teen Challenge, my kids were too young to fully understand so I told them, "Daddy was going to a place to learn about God and ask Him to help me learn how to live a healthier life." And that's just what happened. But make no mistake, it was the most difficult thing I have ever done. I missed my wife and kids every day. I had to give up every bit of control over my life but I had no other options. Every other way of living had failed, horribly. I knew that if I left the program, I would die. And I began, finally, to let God work in my life.

For the first time in my life,
I surrendered and gave God control.

That was over eight years ago, He is still in control today, and I am still a part of Teen Challenge! I remember hearing a pastor say once, when someone asked how long the program was, he said, "The rest of your life."

I can tell you, I am a different man today. I have meaning and purpose and I am happy to be alive. I graduated from the Teen Challenge Brockton program and completed Bible courses at Global University and received a certificate in Biblical Counseling. I also became a Licensed Minister. My professional experience with computers allowed me to become the Director of Technology for Teen Challenge New England, Inc. I am currently enrolled in a Master's program in seminary. I am able to preach and teach as well as counsel the students and the staff. As wonderful of an opportunity as it has been to be a part of the Teen Challenge family and to help others, God did not stop there. For over five years, I have been the pastor of my church. That's right, not two miles from where I used to lead others into darkness, I now lead them into the light and warmth of God's love.

I am grateful for everything now. I can often be heard saying "No better life," because that is my experience and my conclusion. I tried everything to fill the void, yet peace remained out of reach. That's when some really good people began to shine the light of Christ in my life. It has made all of the difference. I tell people that life with Jesus can still be hard, but life without Jesus was much harder! My wife and I get along better than we ever have. I spend lots of time with my kids and my focus is on them and their lives. I am no longer distracted and inattentive. I remember the day that my daughter told me that even though she missed me when I was away at "God school," she likes me a lot better now and she says, "God helped her daddy."

Ephesians 3:20 says that God is able to do "immeasurably more than we can ask or imagine." I wouldn't have believed that, except that I am living proof! I just needed to surrender. One of my favorite quotes by Fitzgerald used to be, "Show me a hero and I will write you a tragedy". But God showed me that with Him as our hero, there are always happy endings. I just needed to be willing to trust Him. He will use "...all things for good" Romans 8:28. Best of all, I no longer feel that void. I am filled, at peace and live a life most richly blessed. Thank you Jesus and thank you Teen Challenge!

Edited by David B. King

Chapter 9
Changing Tracks

Keith LaFleur

A Runner is Born

On July 26th 1977, I was born in the town of Winchester, Massachusetts. My family situation was a challenging one because my parents did not remain in a committed relationship after I was born. My father was in and out and left my mother struggling to make ends meet. Several years later, my mother met the man she would eventually marry and my family's situation became more positive. My mother and Walter eventually married. My mother's father offered my parents management positions in his restaurant in Marion, Massachusetts. The family moved to Marion where we lived for several years, but eventually we moved to Wareham, Massachusetts where I lived most of my life. From a very early age, it seemed I was running from one place to the next.

My childhood was very busy. My days were filled with

camping, sports, and family events. My parents were always there for me. They taught me right from wrong, provided discipline, and encouraged me when I faced obstacles. When I turned nine years old, I signed up for peewee football. I also played organized league basketball. I loved to play team sports because they made me feel like I belonged to something bigger and I was accepted by my peers. Through the training regimen, I developed a love for running. I absolutely loved to run and I excelled at it. One of the most exciting times of the year for me was field day. I loved to compete against the fastest kids in my grade and beat them in a race. By the time is was in sixth grade, I was running 10K road races and winning my age division. I have many fond memories of my adolescent years. However, the next phase of my life would lead me down a path I would never have imagined.

A New Run Begins

In September of 1992, I became a freshman in high school. Like most people, I felt I was walking into a whole new world. I remember simultaneously feeling a sense of fear of the unknown and excitement! The second week of school I was introduced to the cross country coach who also happened to be the varsity basketball coach. I signed up for the cross country team that day and it did not take long for the coaches to notice that I had a natural talent for running. I ran cross-country and winter and spring track for the first two years of high school. All seemed to be going well. I performed well academically and I had a steady girlfriend. Unfortunately, there was something lurking underneath the surface that not everyone could see at the time. For roughly two years, I had been smoking marijuana secretly. As I headed into my junior year, I was a star athlete. My popularity at school was peaking and academically I was preparing for entry into college. That's when the enemy hit me squarely with the very thing that would take me down. Alcohol came running into this runner's life.

Of course when I started drinking I did not think that I would turn into a full-blown alcoholic. Do we ever think that awful things will happen to us? I would drink during the weekend with friends at their houses or out in the woods. That same year I was introduced to other drugs like acid and psychedelic mushrooms. At this point, the people around me began to see me change for the worst. Many became concerned about the direction I was headed. My grade point average declined and my interest in sports diminished. I entered my senior year with virtually no concern for athletics. My relationship with my longtime girlfriend had ended and I found myself dangerously close to not having enough credits to graduate. I did not realize it at the time, but I was a full- blown addict at the age of 18!

At this point my mother interjected herself into my academic situation and established a plan that allowed me to graduate with my class. Sadly though, this small glimmer of hope faded rapidly and I continued on the path of destruction. I thought I was done with running after completing high school. Ironically, life was about to show me what it truly means to run.

Running for my Life

Upon graduation, I moved to North Andover, Massachusetts in order to work for my uncle Tom's company. Initially things went very well but once I located the parties, I drank every night. My work ethic went out the window and my grandmother asked me to move out. I tried to improve my family relationships but in the end I had to leave because my drinking was interfering with everything. I moved back into my parent's house in the hopes that things would change for the better.

After several months my mother sat down to talk to me regarding money my grandfather left as inheritance for his children and grandchildren. When I heard about the money, I was very excited. I thought that this would be the start of better things for me. I called a meeting with some old friends to celebrate my good fortune and to discuss possible investment ideas for the funds. That night changed the course of my life in a way that I could never have imagined.

That evening I entered into the dangerous world of drug distribution. I fell in league with a pack of wolves. My friends and I sold every drug you could think of during this period of time. I became involved with the high-level distribution of heroin to mid-level street dealers. I choose to sell heroin because it was not my drug of choice. These transactions were extremely advantageous financially. I began using cocaine and ecstasy on top of drinking. After a time, I became disillusioned with drug dealing and my life style choice. My friends were unaware that I had spent the bulk of my inheritance and only had a few thousand dollars remaining from drug sales. One day I decided to leave and I bought a ticket and headed to Burlington, Vermont. I found employment quickly in Burlington and fell right into the social crowd of the city. With a fresh start, my situation improved and I felt like I had made a good decision. My drinking continued however and soon the downward spiral began.

I lost my job and my apartment.
For the first time in my life I was officially homeless.

I was financially busted, morally broke and had completely lost my way. I spent a short time in Florida, but was soon back in Massachusetts, hoping for another chance with my family.

Once I settled in at home, my situation improved rather quickly. Life seemed good again. The girl I fell in love with in high school walked back into my life. The final installment of my inheritance had arrived so I purchased a new vehicle. I found employment quickly; everything was coming together. This time it would be different. Several months elapsed and my girlfriend informed me that she wanted to move out of state with her aunt. I thought that by agreeing to the request I was being a good boyfriend and we decided to make the long distance relationship work the best that we could. That move was the beginning of the end of the relationship. In the next three and a half years my drinking and cocaine usage increased exponentially. In the end I pushed her away just like I had done to everybody in my life that loved me. I found myself once again with no job, no girlfriend, no money, and homeless. I thought every day was a party. I slept on couches, in cars, and in a tent in the middle of winter. This lifestyle became acceptable to me.

A year later, opportunity came knocking and I saw a chance to improve my situation once again. My aunt Debbie was in need of some construction work on her house. I moved to the town of Wilmington, Massachusetts to help my aunt with the project for a few weeks. Two weeks turned into two years. I lived in a trailer next door to my aunt and worked for people in the neighborhood. This time my situation did not improve. After a serious altercation over cocaine with a local drug dealer, I left Wilmington that night. My mission was to try

to yet again improve my situation. I did not know that the decision to leave would change my life dramatically. In track it was running the final lap. Little did I know that it would be the last lap for me in this race.

The Running Ends

The next morning I found myself wandering around the beautiful town of Wakefield, Massachusetts. I had nowhere to go and I had no idea of what I was going to do. I spent the rest of my money on beer and cigarettes. It started to get late and with nowhere to sleep, I decided to head into an old cemetery that I walked by earlier that day. By the third night in the cemetery, I was totally paranoid and plagued with thoughts of people coming after me. I was hiding behind head stones and suffered from thoughts of suicide. I felt my life slipping away from me. The realization of my situation became clear to me. I needed help. I started to pray to a God I never knew!

I fell asleep under a tree and I woke the next morning on a mission to get some help. That morning I remembered that my mother had told me about a program nearby. I called her to see if she would help me get into it. Once I talked to my mother, I felt I was close to the finish line. I had been running for years but it was almost over. When Mom picked me up, I was in really bad shape. I was in desperate need of food and even greater need of a shower. We went to a sub shop and it was there I found out how badly I had hurt my body; I could not hold down any food and I was shaking.

During the ride to Brockton, Massachusetts my mother made a very simple request of me that I never forgot. She asked me to keep an open mind when it came to the Christian part of the program. She asked me to let the people help me with my issues. Those requests will stay with me for the rest of my life because they altered my life forever. When we arrived at the Teen Challenge Brockton, I felt as if I was at the end of myself but soon after I knew I was home. I went through the intake process and I was ushered to the dorms for much needed personal hygiene. That was the best shower I had ever taken! The last thing I remember about that day was heading to bed. That night was the best night's sleep I'd had in years.

The New Race

The next day I woke up with a joy and peace I had not felt in years. I could not explain why, but all I knew was, I liked it! Like my mother has asked, I kept an open mind about the Christian part of the program. My first experience in a corporate prayer session was different but went well. By lunch time, I was able to keep food down and began to feel better physically. I was corrected during campus clean up because of my foul language and from that point on my swearing stopped.

God revealed himself to me that afternoon.

I realized that I had no desire to drink. I did not want to smoke. I physically felt great and I felt an inward peace that I could not explain.

My next thought was, there is no way that this program could be this good. There must be a God! In that moment the Lord spoke to my heart and said "Welcome home." The very next week, we had a six hour prayer vigil led by Pastor Jimmy Lilley and that is when I gave my whole life to Jesus!

At the end of my second week, I was selected to work at the carwash ministry. From the very first day, I loved the carwash. God knew the right group of leaders that I needed to be around. Throughout those fourteen months I learned the power of prayer and of intercession for people around me. I learned how to be a responsible person and how to lead others by implementing biblical principles. As my fourteenth month approached, the leadership transferred me to the thrift store where I became a delivery driver. I was not happy about the move but God taught me how to trust the leadership that he places over us. My leader was Pastor Pete Raftery and he was a wonderful influence for me as he constantly encouraged myself and others through God's word. Consequently, I found a deep love for the word of God during my six months at the thrift store. This had a deep impact on my devotional life and assisted my growing intimately closer to God. This was the first of many lessons in leadership training and personal character refinement that I learned through my various positions in Teen Challenge. The Lord soon made me aware that he was calling me to fulltime ministry and that everything he was teaching me would help me as a leader.

I developed discernment to learn how to work with individual students and my peers in leadership. Working with the program supervision team, I learned what it takes to manage the program. I learned to communicate more effectively. I learned to delegate and how to discipline. My time management skills improved. In the learning center, I fell in love with the academics. I was able to work directly with the students and advance their biblical knowledge. This was very exciting for me because I love to teach God's word. It brings me great joy to see His word transform minds and change people's actions. I also had the great pleasure of working with one of the Lord's great servants, Pastor Lilley. He had a profound impact on my spiritual leadership. I was able to positively impact the students and counsel them from a biblical standpoint. This was one of the best times I had in Teen Challenge. I thought that it could never get better than this. Little did I know that God was preparing me for something more than I could have imagined.

The New Race Continues

I had served at Teen Challenge Brockton for six years. All this time I knew God had called me to work with people that were as lost and hopeless as I had been. Soon I was asked to be the Program Supervisor for the Brockton Campus. I worked closely with the Associate Director, Oscar Cruz. While working with him I could not help but notice his calm demeanor and his steady tone during the most intense situations. I needed this example of meekness and he displayed it in the truest form.

One year later, I was asked to pray about transferring to Maine to be the Associate Director. All weekend I prayed about the situation but I did not feel the Lord leading me in any direction. On Monday morning I spoke to a good friend of mine and he asked about my decision. I told him that for the first time I may have to tell my leadership "no! " After he left the room, something did not feel right. I continued to pray. I heard the Lord speak to me loud and clear. He said "Keith, it does not feel right because you are fighting against what I want you to do." God used many people to speak to me and by the end of the day I had received my answer. There was no doubt as to the direction I was to take.

I arrived in Maine two years ago and my journey has been amazing. I have had the privilege to serve under Executive Director Steve Gadomski's leadership and the opportunity to serve the men in Maine. I received my license with the Assemblies of God and am currently finishing my ordination level studies. I anticipate enrolling in undergraduate studies for a degree in psychology this fall. The Lord has been so good to me. Only by his intense love and saving grace are any of these opportunities possible. I will continue to run this race and live this life of faith until He calls me home. It is never too late to give your life to the one who gave His all for you. It is never too late to change the race you are running in your life. Change the track and you change your life.

Chapter 10
All In

Michael P. Hayes-Moore

My name is Michael P. Hayes-Moore and I grew up on the Jersey Shore in Bayville, New Jersey. I was born on August 26, 1977. I am the oldest of six siblings. I have two younger brothers and triplet sisters.

For the majority of my childhood I was raised by an abusive, alcoholic step-father that I thought was my real father. I didn't find out until age 12 that he wasn't my real father. I felt deceived and really couldn't understand why I was led to believe that this man was my real father. I remember thinking, where is my real father and why did he leave me? Needless to say, I dealt with serious abandonment issues at a very young age. I also experienced and saw a lot of physical, mental, and emotional abuse. I didn't like to be home, so I picked up the sport of skateboarding to escape my house. I would also play street basketball late into the night. But my greatest escape came from playing soccer. My first soccer coach was a man named Frank Penevolpe. Frank became a father figure to me throughout my childhood. He picked me up for every practice and game. He poured his life into mine because he saw the need. Frank was a deacon in our local church, Emmanuel Baptist Church in Bayville, New Jersey. Frank would pick me up every Sunday for church. I gave my life to the Lord at the age of 12 years old.

My mother did everything she could to support and protect us. After my step-father moved out, we really had to work hard to make ends meet. My mom worked as a bus driver and sometimes we were left home alone. The responsibility for caring for my brothers fell to me. It was during this time that I lost my "Nanny" due to alcoholism and my uncle, who also struggled with addiction, committed suicide. I was close to both of them and losing them was very difficult for me.

For most of my teenage years I resorted to crime to help the family and bring food into the house. I stopped going to church and fell away from God. I was introduced to some friends who were also from broken homes. We all could relate to each other in many ways and as a result became very tight. We would break into cars and steal from various stores. My friends were also into alcohol and drugs and many of them were even dealing drugs on a large scale. I never touched alcohol or drugs during my high school years because I felt what happened in my family would happen to me.

My mother met her second husband when I was 16 years old. They got married on May 10, 1994 and he moved into our home. It was very difficult to have another man in the house since I was used to taking care of a lot of things. My new stepfather and I didn't always see eye to eye, but we managed to get along for the most part.

During my high school years I was able to avoid trouble during soccer season but made up for it in the off season. I loved to make everyone laugh and I was voted class clown in the 6th, 8th, and 12th grade year books. But I don't know if that's an accomplishment or not. I do know that I used it as a coping mechanism for all that was going on in my home life. When I was 16 years old, I was arrested for breaking into cars and at 17 years old for stealing from a store.

My senior year in high school was full of ups and downs. My high school had a point system for infractions and this was one area in my life where my high score would hurt me as many of my infractions were class clown antics that I took too far. If a student accumulated too many points, eventually they were expelled from school. I had about three months left in my senior year and I was about to get expelled.

I was being contacted by colleges to play soccer at their schools. There was one school in particular that accepted me despite my grades and behavior. That school was

Rowan University in Glassboro, New Jersey. Coach Gilmore was known for taking risks with troubled high school kids with talent. I was poised to be the second person in my family to go to college but my expulsion could ruin my opportunity. My mother and I had a meeting with the superintendent, principal and my high school coach, Rob Bechtloff, to discuss my situation. The superintendent was a no-nonsense, zero-tolerance type of school administrator.

> She wanted to expel me from school because of the number of points for infractions that I had accumulated.

I will never forget how Coach Beck spoke up for me. He explained that I just gotten accepted to Rowan University and it wouldn't make any sense to expel me from school and ruin my life. After some convincing, she agreed that if I didn't get one infraction for the remaining three months of school, that I could graduate. I must admit I was surprised and relieved. If it wasn't for Coach Beck I would have been expelled my senior year. I did manage to not get any points during the last three months, but just barely. I graduated from high school and spent most of my summer working from morning to night and I believe that helped me to stay out of trouble. I knew that I had been given a great opportunity to attend college and I did not want to squander it.

While it was extremely difficult to leave my house and friends, I realize it was the best thing for me. My friends were into some serious drug dealing and crime. If I stayed in my town I would have ended up in prison like many of them did. My friends were having their houses raided by the cops and they were in and out of jail. It was obvious that they weren't a good influence on me.

Because I was on the soccer team, I had to arrive early at college for preseason training. Nothing could have prepared me for what I was about to face. Coach Gilmore is legendary for being one of the toughest, hardnosed college soccer coaches in America. He is also one of the winningest coaches. Coach Gilmore's conditioning was the toughest most strenuous thing I ever had to face up to that point in my life.

Despite being terribly homesick, I quickly became acclimated to college life and made a lot of friends. I was used to being at parties and not drinking or drugging. I had resolved to stay sober because I saw how it destroyed my family and many of my friends. I also wanted to play professional soccer and I knew that drinking and drugging would destroy that dream. I've seen some of my soccer friends flunk out and move on because of drinking and drugging. I've seen talented men never reach their potential because of drugs.

My freshmen year was time of change and growing up. Mostly I played soccer. I scored the first goal of the season and started most of the games that year. Our team went undefeated but lost in the first rounds of the NCAA tournament. I made a lot of close friends on that team that I still speak with to this day.

My first encounter with any type of drug happened my freshmen year after soccer season. I remember being in my dorm room and someone brought out a smoking device for marijuana. For some reason I decided to try marijuana for the first time. After I smoked I felt very strange. I had never put anything in my body before so it really affected me. I still felt the effects the next day. I didn't want anyone to know that I had smoked marijuana, so I kept it a secret for a long time.

College life went on and I didn't smoke marijuana again or drink until my junior year. During my junior year, I lived in what's called a "soccer house." It was a house off the college campus full of seven soccer players. I was 20 years old and had my first drink of alcohol. My longtime girlfriend and I had broken up so I used that as my excuse. Once I got a taste of alcohol, I quickly became a big partier. I also used other drugs during this time. It became a way for me to cope with an emptiness that I always had inside. I know now that the emptiness I was experiencing was because I was separated from God.

I was able to keep things together and function enough to pass my courses during that junior year. The following summer, my partying became more intense. I was hanging out

with old friends and getting into trouble. I had many encounters with the law because of my friends and their actions. The cops would ask me why I was hanging out with these guys when I had a bright future. Good question! Despite my partying, I still trained very hard to prepare for my upcoming senior year's soccer season.

Unfortunately, my partying almost took my life when one night I chose to drink and drive. I was headed home after a night out in Seaside Heights, New Jersey and I took a detour to go see a friend. It was late and I was speeding down a side street. Before I realized it, I ran a stop sign. I slammed on the brakes and skidded into a brick wall in front of a house, totaling my car. I fled the scene and ran from house to house, hiding. I even swam across a portion of the bay in Island Heights, New Jersey, and almost drowned. My brother Patrick found out about the accident and went looking for me. He found me a couple miles away and I turned myself in the next day. They only charged me with leaving the scene of an accident. I know that God saved me that day and I believe that it was a warning that I unfortunately did not heed.

My drinking got progressively worse during my senior year in college.

> I found a reason to drink almost every night.

During the soccer season I kept it together enough to make a successful effort. As the captain, I helped lead our team to the Final Four. I was voted All-American and played in the Umbro-Select All Star Game in Florida. I even had a chance to play professional soccer locally for the South Jersey Barons.

I graduated college and started working as a Health and Physical Education teacher in Mt. Laurel, New Jersey. For the first two years of teaching, things went very well. I didn't party as much and I was really focused on teaching and coaching. I had also landed a job as the Head Varsity Soccer Coach at Bishop Eustace Preparatory School. My first year coaching we won the conference and went to the state finals. I was running my own soccer camps and directing soccer camps for Adidas Coerver.

I started to drink heavily during my third year of teaching. I had another break up and began to hang out with the wrong crowd again. I was arrested for disorderly conduct and drinking in public. I also got my second DWI (Driving While Intoxicated) around this time. I crashed a car but still made it to work the next day. The secretary at the school smelled alcohol on my breath and told the principal. I got called to the principal's office and I admitted to drinking the night before. He told me to take some time off to get things right. Shortly after that, I went to a 30 day rehabilitation program in Jacksonville,

Florida. After coming out of the program, I went and stayed with my mother. She needed help with my triplet sisters and at that time I thought it would be best to be with family.

I ended up resigning my position despite the Board of Education requesting that I come back to teach. I stayed sober about three months. I started drinking and drugging worse than I ever did before. I would take a bus to Atlantic City and stay down there for days. I found myself in some very dangerous situations in very deadly areas. At that time I really didn't care if I lived or died. I felt like I had no hope and that I had lost everything.

It was only a matter of time before my step-father and mother had enough of my drinking and drugging. They told me I had to leave. I became the king of couch surfing and stayed with many different people. I was in and out of jail and psych wards. I was also in and out of rehabilitation programs. I tried everything to get sober because I knew I didn't want to live the way I was living anymore. I was doing things I never thought I would do. I was trying every type of drug on top of excessive drinking. My life was out of control and in desperate need of a change.

I was on probation and violated probation numerous times. I got picked up in January 2009 by the sheriff for an outstanding warrant. I spent about 30 days in jail before they released me. They said I was going to do six months, but the next day in court I was released. I remember it was close to the weekend and I returned to where I was living. They told me that I wasn't allowed to live there anymore, so I went on one last run with my cousin and her boyfriend.

I ended up at a bus station in Toms River, New Jersey. I will never forget crying out to God and asking Him to save me. As I look back to that time in my life, I think of these verses in Psalm 40:1-2, "I waited patiently for the Lord; he turned to me and heard my cry. He lifted me out of the slimy pit, out of the mud and mire; he set my feet on a rock and gave me a firm place to stand." I took a bus to my mother's house in Barnegat, New Jersey. As I walked through my mother's door, I could see the look of shock on her face. My triplet sisters ran and hugged me. My mom said I needed to talk with Tito, my step-father, about staying there. When I spoke with Tito, he told me I needed to leave or he would call the cops. Although at the time this was very hurtful, I now know this was part of God's plan.

As I walked out of the house my brother's girlfriend stopped me and asked where I was going. I said I didn't know, maybe Atlantic City. She then told me that my brother was in a program called Teen Challenge in New Haven, Connecticut. At first, I thought that my brother was a counselor at a place for teenagers. As we talked, it became clear that he was in a Christian program. She told me that they had been praying for

me for the past 30 days.

> At that moment it all added up and I knew it was an answer from God.

We called the intake coordinator, and the next day I was on a bus to New Haven, Connecticut.

I came through the doors of Teen Challenge Connecticut on February 25, 2009. The first person I saw was my brother. I've been through different types of programs but nothing like what was in store for me at Teen Challenge. As tough as the program was, it was everything God knew I needed; discipline, structure, and Christ at the center. Back when I went through the program, at the six month mark, we were transferred to Brockton, Massachusetts. I thought I would serve at the thrift store since I trained for six months at the thrift store in Connecticut. I was wrong.

Instead, I spent six months at the car wash. It was ten hours a day, seven days a week through all kinds of inclement weather. I had a choice to make while I was there and I chose to be all in with God and press in like never before. Only Jesus got me through those six months and the rest of my time in the program. I took the curriculum very seriously. I read every book I could get my hands on, especially the Bible. I was studying my Bible and praying all the time. I had given everything else in my life a chance, so I thought, why not God? I grew a lot through my time in Teen Challenge. I transferred back to the Connecticut center in February of 2010. The director asked me to manage the thrift store. This was a very difficult task. I prayed and asked God for help to be able to handle this huge responsibility.

A little while after being asked to be the manager of the thrift store, the center director got sick and Rick Welch became the Executive Director of Connecticut. Pastor Rick and I quickly connected. The one word that I would use to describe him is authentic. He has taught me so much and has been patient with me. I owe him a lot of thanks and gratitude for pouring into me all the time.

The ministry began the implementation of the Emerging Leaders Program (ELP) for the internship. I was one of the first interns to complete the ELP program. I commenced the Teen Challenge 15 month program in May of 2010 and finished ELP in November 2011. Then I was hired as a staff member at Teen Challenge Connecticut.

There have been times when I contemplated moving on but now I look back and see why God has kept me here in Teen Challenge. One blessing was meeting my beautiful wife. For two years I prayed specifically about a wife, asking God to give me exactly whom he had for me. I met Aimee Moore in February 2012 through Christian Mingle. Yes, God used

Christian Mingle! Aimee and I decided to meet up at church and then went on a super date to Bertucci's, Barnes and Noble, the mall, movies, and Starbucks. We didn't want the date to end. I knew right away that she was going to be my wife. I wondered how I could talk her into marrying me.

We dated for a little while before I asked Aimee to be my wife on December 15, 2012. I asked her at Rockefeller Center in front of the Christmas tree. We quickly planned our wedding, went through couples counseling and pastoral counseling with our officiant. I was growing closer and closer to my future mother and father in law, Rod and Sue Moore, who have treated me like a son from day one. I greatly appreciate them as well as my sister in law, Allison Moore.

Aimee and I were married on May 26, 2013. It was a dream come true to marry the woman God gave me in front of family and close friends. Only God could have put Aimee and I together. Being married brings to mind two scripture verses: Mark 10:7-9 "For this reason a man will leave his father and mother and be united to his wife and the two will become one flesh. So they are no longer two, but one flesh. Therefore what God has joined together, let no one separate." and Proverbs 18:22 "He who finds a wife finds what is good and receives favor from the Lord." As I write my story, Aimee and I have just celebrated two years of marriage.

> I don't ever want to forget that God took me from the gutter to make a difference for his kingdom.

God continues to use me in the ministry of Teen Challenge. Currently, I am the Assistant Director for Teen Challenge Connecticut. I have finished my first level to be a certified minister and now I am a credentialed pastor with the Assemblies of God. I am amazed at what God has done! This is an absolute miracle! The scripture that comes to mind is Romans 12:1-2-1 "Therefore, I urge you, brothers and sisters, in view of God's mercy, to offer your bodies as a living sacrifice, holy and pleasing to God—this is your true and proper worship. Do not conform to the pattern of this world, but be transformed by the renewing of your mind. Then you will be able to test and approve what God's will is—his good, pleasing and perfect will."

I just want to please God and stay in His will no matter what. I don't know what the future holds, but He does, and I am all in with Jesus. I am very grateful for what God has done in my life and how He is using me in the ministry. He has truly changed me into a new person. Since Christ came into my life, there has been a metamorphosis, a radical change in my life!

I know I have a long way to go but I am on the right

godly road. My hope is that I leave a Christ-like legacy wherever I go. I would like to thank Jesus Christ my Lord and Savior for coming into my life and saving me. I would also like to thank Edith Padilla, Pastor Jose, and Pastor Rick, Teen Challenge Connecticut, my wife Aimee, and anyone else who had a hand in changing my life.

With the love of Christ,
Michael P. Hayes-Moore

Chapter 11
Fifteen Months Seemed Like Forever

Michael Goff

Within the last couple of years, I learned that my parents had a difficult time having children. My mother was one of the first women in Massachusetts to use In Vitro Fertilization. When I learned this, it opened my eyes. I can't image trying and hoping to have a baby, spending time and money, countless appointments, and then having to sit back and watch their child make life-threatening decisions. I knew my mother loved me, and I knew that I had been killing her with my lifestyle, realizing this made it even more painful for me.

When I was four years old, my mom became pregnant with my brother Tim. It was discovered that he would be born with severe disabilities. This was a huge challenge for everyone, but it was not going to change. We had to learn to adapt and be a family.

I don't remember a lot from my early childhood, but I do

remember that it seemed like my brother was getting a lot of attention. I couldn't understand why everything that my brother did was a huge accomplishment when I did all the same stuff and nobody seemed to notice. My mother would try to explain that he was special and it was harder for him to do all the things I did easily, but it just made me angry and jealous. I don't think I can describe how hard it was for me to live with my brother. Everywhere we went people stared at us all the time. Usually because he was making a scene and it felt like my family was a circus show. I was so embarrassed; I wanted a normal brother so badly. Even though we were four years apart, we went to the same school. I was horrified to see him in the cafeteria because I didn't want anyone to know he was my brother. I was very harsh towards him and would come to regret the way that I treated him.

When I was nine years old, my parents separated. This wasn't a shock to me because they fought all the time. I told them many times that they should just get a divorce and stop fighting but that didn't ease the blow when they finally sat down and told me. I think part of the reason I resented my brother is that I thought he was the reason my parents were splitting up. My father had no clue what to do with my brother. I think he tried but seriously lacked the ability to relate to him in a way that was effective and nurturing.

> Now that my parents were getting a divorce, I was hurt because it meant that my father would be gone.

Even though he treated my mother and brother badly, he was a decent father to me. We would play ball and he coached some of my baseball teams. I think I was the only thing in his life that felt normal--the same way him taking me to baseball felt normal to me. Now that he was gone, I felt like my life became even more different from my peers. I was the only one with a special needs brother and then I became one of the first to have divorced parents.

I remember being angry and feeling like I got cheated. My attitude was bad and my mother and brother received the brunt of my bad behavior. My mother knew that I was hurting and tried hard to get me help. She knew she couldn't be a father so she tried to have positive male role models in my life spend time with me. Sometimes it would work and sometimes I wasn't interested. She got me into counseling which never really went well. Honestly, it was just one more thing for me to be miserable about. I don't think my mother thought things could get much worse, but they did.

About a year after my father moved out, he was involved in an event that shocked everyone who knew him. He was arrested for assault. It wasn't because he was angry or violent as much as he had a breakdown. Because it was a mental issue, he was sentenced to Taunton State Hospital in Taunton, Massachusetts for punishment. We weren't seeing my father on a regular basis, but my mother did take me to visit him a couple times while he was there. This place was easily the scariest place I had ever been. It was like a horror movie come to life and it terrified me.

My father was released a few years later, but things would never be the same. This incident affected me for the next ten years. With my father gone, my mother worked hard to keep life as normal as possible, but she had many things to deal with. I started to misbehave. When I would get in trouble, she was good at disciplining me but looking back, I probably needed a father to put fear into me and she couldn't do that. She really couldn't hurt me. I started to talk back, get in trouble at school, and stopped doing homework. That is when things began to fall apart.

In middle school, I was not a good student academically, I got detention occasionally, and went to the principal's office sometimes. I got caught shop lifting stupid stuff from a department store and I tried smoking cigarettes. I wasn't doing drugs or drinking though. I was far from the worst kid, but I was on a path that was leading to real challenges and trouble.

My freshman and sophomore years of high school went well. I went to class, got C's and I didn't get into much trouble.

The summer between my sophomore and junior year, I started smoking marijuana every day. I loved it. It was an escape from everything that was going on around me. I wasn't a good student, I wasn't "going places", I was just there. Smoking was what I looked forward to when I woke up in the morning.

At first my friends and I partied hard just on weekends but soon we started to live like that every day. I can't remember a day at school that went by when I wasn't high or drunk. I can't remember classes, taking tests, doing reports, anything. It all stopped. I went to school to see friends or I would skip classes for weeks. I had an after school job at Kentucky Fried Chicken. This was a dream job at the time because all my friends got hired as cooks, so every shift was like a party. This was the one thing that I was doing right, but it didn't last.

One night, the safe was left open in the office.
I took $250 and hid it so I could steal it later.

The managers realized that money was missing and shut the place down at closing. They didn't find the money and the next day some friends and I skipped school to drink and smoke marijuana. When I got home that afternoon, my manager had called and told my mother what happened. She took me to work and I confessed that I had taken the money. I remember them saying if I gave them the money back there would be no charges. I only had $11 left. My manager looked at me in disgust and told me I had a drug problem and would be locked up sooner rather than later. She was right.

My mother was devastated. I had been stealing from her for years, but this incident crushed her. She knew that I needed to learn a lesson, so she allowed me to deal with the consequences. I was locked up in a youth detention center for the first time as a teen. Probation would follow along with many random drug tests. I tried really hard not to get high because I didn't think it was worth being locked up again, but it didn't work. All my friends were getting high and I couldn't avoid it.

I lived with the constant tension of being caught for the things I was doing. I ended up spending the last six months before I turned 18 years old in detention centers and juvenile drug programs. I couldn't understand how some people could live wild, never get caught and never deal with the consequences. When I turned eighteen I thought I could be like them, no more probation, no more drug tests, and a clean slate. That didn't last long and it was less than six months before I was in trouble again, but this time I was an adult. Detectives were calling my house and talking to me, accusing me of crimes, but never arresting me. That was stressful because I never knew if I would be arrested. I wasn't welcome at home, so I was sleeping wherever I could. I remember telling people my mother had kicked me out and that I was homeless. Realistically I had kicked myself out. Not having a place to stay during the summer wasn't too bad, it was almost fun. Not having a place to stay during New England winters was a different matter. I would do anything to sleep indoors. Some nights I would have to walk around all night or find an unlocked car to sleep in. I remember one bitterly cold night praying to God that I wouldn't freeze to death because I knew it would devastate my mother and brother. Then there was one night when everything started to change.

It was a night in January when the weather was particularly nasty. I didn't want to sleep in a car again so I called my mother's house all night. Finally at three in the morning she answered and said I could come and sleep there. I had to be out by six am because she was leaving for a couple days and I couldn't stay there while she was gone. My bed felt so good that night. It seemed like just minutes later that six o' clock came and I had to leave. It was still freezing outside and I couldn't imagine going back out there with nowhere to go. I was trying to talk my mother into letting me stay when she said she was going to a hotel in Boston, Massachusetts and I could join her if I wanted to. I honestly don't think she wanted to say this, it just happened, and I was all over it.

On the ride up she explained that she was going to a Christian conference, and if I was going, I had to attend church with her. I would have agreed to anything; I just wanted food and a place to sleep. When I got there we met up with a woman from the church I had grown up in. She was so kind to me even though she knew everything that was going on. I went to church with them though my mindset was completely anti-God. I remember laughing at the speaker, in a good way. I'm not sure if I had ever laughed in church before, but it felt good. Then I bumped into a man that I had known when I was an early teen. This guy had really tried to love me and be there for me. I hadn't seen him in years. When he saw me, he told me I looked like hell. I never heard him talk like that, so I was kind of shocked, but he was right. Somehow I thought things weren't that bad, but in reality, I was a total mess. We had lunch together and he encouraged me to go to Teen Challenge.

Teen Challenge wasn't new to me. People had been trying to get me to go there since I was 16 years old. I always knew that if I got locked up I would be out in less time than if I went to Teen Challenge, so I never went. Now the thought of going there began to feel right. I wasn't sure what was going to happen when I was finally charged in court but I figured it had to be at least an 18-month sentence. Thinking it seemed like a decent option, I called Teen Challenge Brockton the following Monday. A week later I was there for an intake appointment and entered Teen Challenge Boston.

Day one was brutal; this was the last place I wanted to be.

> Fifteen months seemed like forever and this was much different than the other programs I had been in.

As days went on though, it started to seem not so bad. There were a lot of days in the beginning when I wanted to quit, but there were some good people there who convinced me to stay. This thought hit me early on, I remember looking around at men in their 40's and 50's and thinking that I didn't want their life. I didn't want to waste my life or wake up one day having to try and get it together. Before the courts stipulated that I had to finish the program that thought really kept me fighting to stay.

I was at Teen Challenge for about six weeks before my mother got a summons for me to attend court. I had no idea what was going to happen. At this point, I was starting to take Christianity seriously. There was a big part of me that really wanted to get my life together. The thought of having to go to jail instead of being in Teen Challenge scared me, because I knew that I would revert back to my old self when I got out. I was stressed about going to court, so some of the guys in the program prayed with me before I left the center. Their prayer was simple, "God, we know you are working in

Mike's life. Please get him back here today. Even if you have to lose his paperwork, just make sure he returns." I went to court that morning and sat there until mid-afternoon. Finally I went to look for my name on the list to see how much longer I would have to wait but they didn't have my paperwork! I knew I was on the list; they had called my name that morning. They looked at me and said, "We must have lost it somehow. Come back in thirty days." This was an important moment for my faith. This was a catalyst for me to say, "God, I want to live for you and serve you for the rest of my life."

I wish it was always that easy to say, "Jesus, I love you and want to serve you." The truth is that this was really hard. Teen Challenge was hard. Living with a variety of people and not being able to live a "normal" life was difficult, but God gave me grace and kept making me new.

God kept me in his protection and peace when my mother had a life-changing stroke. I had been in the program almost nine months at that point and I remember when I got the news from the staff. I didn't even know what a stroke was. They let me call her at the hospital and my aunt picked up. I asked to talk to my mother and she told me my mother couldn't talk. Nothing was making sense, but when she did give her the phone, my mother couldn't say a word. I was crushed. I cried harder than I ever had in my life. I had treated my mother poorly for so long. Now she couldn't speak. There were so many questions. My mother loved God, worked hard, and went through hell in her marriage and with her children. Why this? Why now? However, I soon began to see God's kindness and goodness towards me and my family. If my mother had a stroke when I was getting high, I would have taken her wallet from under the hospital bed. I wouldn't have loved her, prayed for her, sat with her. I could see that my life was really starting to change.

The change was so evident that one day my mother left her purse on the table and left the house to get the mail. When she came back in, I asked her what she was thinking. She hadn't left her purse around me in years. She said that God changed my life and she could trust me. The level of grace, trust, and responsibility in my life grew so much. I went from stealing anything I could to being my brother's legal co-guardian and having access to all of my mother's bank accounts. This was a whole new life.

Upon graduation from Teen Challenge Boston, I decided to stay on as staff and serve with the ministry for three years.

> This was a chance to give back to the program and try to help other people who were hurting, the same way that the staff had helped me.

There were so many beautiful experiences in that time, but looking back two things really stand out. First, I learned to love people. I can't believe how hard it was for me to really care about people. I wanted to change that and I believe striving to put others before myself changed something in my soul and continues today. By the grace of God I love people more now than I did in the past. The second thing was developing a passion for preaching and teaching the Bible. I love this. I didn't see this coming, but I experience great joy getting to tell people about Jesus. I currently work at a small church and I have the honor of teaching about the Biblical Jesus every week. This is easily the highlight of my week and it all started because of Teen Challenge.

After a little over four years in Teen Challenge, I applied to Zion Bible College (Currently Northpoint). I remember my first days on campus being in awe that this was the reality of my life. I'm sure that no one saw Bible College in my future! Those four years were filled with many precious moments. I started dating my wife, Heather, and got married three years later. I learned from some great professors and interned with some wonderful churches.

The last church I interned with hired me after graduation to work with unchurched teens at an outreach center. This was a dream job because it was like I was working with fifteen-year-old versions of myself. The goal of the ministry was to provide a safe place for teens to spend Friday nights and to tell them about Jesus. It was this opportunity that brought me to Manchester, New Hampshire where my wife and I would end up starting a church.

In early 2012 we started services for Great Exchange Church. I could not believe this was really happening. We had a small group of people who wanted to see the gospel change our city. We had no clue how to lead a church. But we wanted to tell people that God is incredibly gracious and good, and we have been doing just that. It is an incredible privilege to be able to do this, and I am very grateful God that called me.

This is my life now. I'm not sure where else the journey is going, but it has been and will always be an adventure. I am so blessed, and honestly feel unworthy, to be able to do this with Heather. She knows the best and the worst version of me and still loves and forgives me. I see the grace and love of God in the way she interacts with me. When I am stressed out and overwhelmed, she walks beside me until I experience the peace of God again. When I am way ahead of myself, she grounds me and pulls me back to reality. When I think too highly of myself, she knows how to humble me. Right behind the cross, she will always be the greatest gift in my life, and I feel so loved by God because He let her love me.

My mother has been a gift as well. No one really knows what God did in my life besides her. She lived it and now can worship God and thank him for changing my life and restoring our relationship. Just today, as I write this, she texted me and said, “Congrats on being ten years out of Teen Challenge. Look what God has done!” She prayed for me all the time, and God heard her prayers.

My brother Tim is turning thirty next year. He lives in Boston, Massachusetts; works at Trader Joe’s and volunteers at the MSPCA (Massachusetts Society for the Prevention of Cruelty to Animals). He is doing so well! The first week of every month he takes the bus up to Manchester, New Hampshire to spend the weekend with Heather and I. He is a big part of our lives. I love my brother today, and I am so grateful I had the chance to grow up with him through all the difficulties. God used those experiences to shape who I am, and I am better because of it.

I can’t wrap this up without thanking God. He made me a son through the death of His Son. I could never understand why God loved me. Then I realized it is only because He is good. There was nothing in me to earn His love. Honestly, there was nothing in me that wanted His love, but He broke through my hard heart and wicked mind and made my sin and Jesus’ death on the cross real to me. I will live for His glory for the rest of my days.

Chapter 12
Help! My Loved One is Addicted!

Allison Cruz

If you have ever found yourself saying, "Help! My loved one is addicted!" then this chapter was written for you. Families can be left without knowing where to turn and what to do, to help their loved one. Families can find themselves exhausted physically, emotionally and spiritually in a situation they feel powerless to change.

Addiction knows no bounds. The faces of addiction include people from all ethnic, social and economic backgrounds. Alcoholism and drug addiction affect a high percentage of the population either directly or indirectly. When addiction affects you directly, it can be very devastating because it not only affects the person who is addicted, but it also has a profound effect on the entire family. Here at Teen Challenge New England & New Jersey, we are dedicated to helping both addicts and their families.

If you have a son, daughter, husband, mother, father, friend or any other loved one who is addicted, you are not alone. When a family faces the pain addiction can bring and their efforts to try and help their loved ones fail, they can be left without knowing where to turn for help. In this situation, it is easy to lose hope, but we're here to tell you that there is always hope. In this chapter we will provide some helpful tips on how to effectively help your loved one who is addicted.

I wish we could understand the "whys" in this world. The reality is that some things, like a mother losing a son or daughter to addiction do not "make sense." It is heartbreaking beyond words to have lost a loved one to addiction.

> I have been forever inspired by mothers who have lost sons and now reach out to help other people's sons and daughters find freedom from addiction.

They are heroes. We are facing an addiction epidemic in our country and our hearts break with all the families who have lost loved ones to this epidemic.

I remember the day I found out my husband was addicted to methamphetamine (meth). My whole world turned upside down in a moment. I tried everything I could to help him, everything from flushing his drugs down the toilet, to throwing his drug paraphernalia in the trash, to begging and pleading with him to get help and attempting to bring him out of the places that he was! He wasn't the same person I married. Meth had taken over his life. There were many sleepless nights spent wondering if he would live another day. I found myself feeling alone with nowhere to turn for help except to God.

During those days, I heard things like: "Go on with your life. You will be fine. Your husband is never going to change." "If your husband is on drugs, I can't help him." Things went from bad to worse and I remember the night I told him that if he went to Teen Challenge and finished the program, that he would have his family back but if he chose drugs, he would lose his family. We had an infant daughter and I knew that it was not safe for us to stay in that situation. I knew he loved us and we loved him, but that night he chose drugs.

In the months to come, I continued to pray and believe that God could restore our family. A year went by and I heard a knock at the door. Oscar, my husband was ready to change! I bought him a one way ticket from Bakersfield to Boston to go into the Teen Challenge Program in Brockton, Massachusetts and they welcomed him with open arms. (You can read Oscar Cruz's story in Changed Lives Book 1.)

Today, he has been free from drugs for over ten years, our daughter has her father back, and our family has been restored from the devastation of addiction! Today he is helping other men find freedom from addiction. I cried out to God for almost four years to save my husband's life and God was faithful.

Even if your loved one has been struggling for decades, change is possible! At Teen Challenge we experience miracles of changed lives on a daily basis. Some say, "Once and addict, always an addict." At Teen Challenge we say, "Addict no more!" The stories in this book are true accounts of real lives that have been changed by the power of God. Teen Challenge New England & New Jersey has helped thousands of alcoholics, addicts and families. You may have found yourself not knowing what do to or how to respond. Gleaned from years of experience working with addicts, we can help you deal with your loved one.

Here are Some Dos and Don'ts

While every situation is different, these tips are to be a general guide on what to do and not do when someone you love is addicted.

Do Love Them - A mother who lost a son to addiction said one of the most important things to do when you have a son or daughter addicted, is to love them. Addicted people are often hard to love because they become a different person. So it becomes important to define what love is in this situation: loving them does not mean enabling them or their addition.

Loving them simply means reminding them that you love and care about them often. You can love someone without loving what they do. Even if they seem unresponsive to the love at the time, they will remember that you love them.

Knowing their family cares about them and that they will be there when they are ready for help can save their life someday. Many times family members are the ones who bring their loved ones to Teen Challenge when they are ready for help.

Do Set Healthy Boundaries - Learning how to set healthy boundaries is one of the most important areas of helping someone who is addicted.

With boundaries, you are able to do everything you can to help your loved one. Without boundaries, your loved one may not realize they have a problem. One of the best examples of setting healthy boundaries is found in the first chapter of Boundaries by Dr. Henry Cloud and Dr. John Townsend. I highly recommend this book to all families dealing with addicted loves ones.

Why is it important to set boundaries? Setting healthy boundaries allows your loved one to experience the consequences of their own actions and choices. When an addict realizes their need for help and takes responsibility for their actions, they are more willing to reach out for help. At Teen Challenge, we call this hitting rock bottom.

If a person who is addicted has everything that they need, a place to live, food, a job, a family that enables them in their addiction, they are most likely not going to hit rock bottom. If they are comfortable in their addiction, the likelihood of reaching out for help can be minimal at best. It is important to emphasize love and care for the addict while at the same time not enabling their addiction. Loving toughness is what is needed in these situations. When you love someone, you set healthy boundaries! Some examples of healthy boundaries are:

Example: You can continue in your addiction if you want to, that is your choice, however, you will not be able to live at home anymore. Our family loves you so much that we cannot support your addiction. When you are ready to receive help, you will be welcome home again.

Example: You can continue in alcoholism or drug use if you want to, but we will not give you any more money to help you with your bills or to support your drinking or drug habit. We care about you and do not want to see you harm yourself anymore.

Example: It is your choice if you want to continue in alcoholism or addiction if you want to, however, it is not a safe situation for the children and you will not be able to live at home or spend time with the children unless you are sober. If you decide to receive help, you will be able to begin rebuilding relationships with your family again. We love you with all our hearts, but this is no longer safe for us.

All of the above examples are difficult, heartbreaking decisions to make. However, when the addict is out of the home, doesn't have money, and can't be around family, they will realize the loss that their addiction has caused, and may reach out for help. If they have everything they want and need, they may not realize that they have a problem.

A person may say, but I love my son, daughter, husband, wife, mother or father, why would I set boundaries like these? We set boundaries because we love them enough to do everything we can to help them. Boundaries also protect you as the family member who has someone struggling.

Boundaries always emphasize personal choices. Both the addict and the family affected have personal choices to make. When a family sets healthy boundaries, many times it is met with great resistance. It is typical for addicts to shift blame from themselves to their families or the people attempting to help them.

Why don't people set healthy boundaries? There are a wide variety of reasons; fear, guilt, a feeling that setting boundaries is not loving, blaming themselves or feeling responsible for their loved ones addiction. Many families have difficulty setting boundaries for fear that it will affect the relationship or that something will happen to their loved one as a result. These are very real fears, but with God's help they can be overcome. No one can tell someone else when to set certain boundaries with their son or daughter. This is a personal choice that should be done with much love and prayer.

Remember, when someone is addicted, they are adversely affecting their health, life and family in many ways and that is their decision. It is not the fault of the family that the loved one is addicted. Each person has personal choices to make and each choice a person makes has consequences. Boundaries help the family to not contribute to the addiction in any way. By settling healthy limits you can help them to reach out for assistance sooner.

Do Seek Support in Church, Support Groups and Counseling - During this time, you need support. When your loved one is struggling, it can be easy to focus all your energy on helping them. Connecting with your local church's pastor, attending a support group for families with addicted loved ones or scheduling an appointment with a counselor to receive professional help can all provide support for you during this time.

Do Self-Care - Life with an addict is like being on a roller coast ride with many curves, ups and downs. It is important to take care of yourself during this time emotionally, physically and spiritually. Families of those addicted seem to exhaust all their resources and energy to help the addict while they themselves are dying on the inside. Self-care is important during this season. Do something fun and recreational, spend time with a good friend, and rest in the presence of God often during this difficult season.

Do Safe Guard Prescriptions, Alcohol or Money - Keep money, valuables, prescription drugs, and alcohol out of reach of the addict. Additionally, it is best if the family of an addict also abstains from all alcohol and recreational drugs to keep the temptation out of reach.

Do Take Safety Precautions - Situations with addicts can quickly become unsafe. If you feel your safety or the safety of others is at risk, take the appropriate action. Call 911 if you are in immediate danger or file for a restraining order with the court if safety is an ongoing concern. Addiction can cause people to do things they would not otherwise do and your safety is important during this time.

Do Protect Affected Children - The most vulnerable people in the situation are children. When a child is living in a home with a parent impaired with a substance, that parent is unable to care for them. Children in substance abuse affected homes are at higher risk of trauma, neglect and abuse and must be kept safe from these dangers. If you know of a child who is in danger, be their voice. It is important for the children to be cared for in a safe and loving environment and not taken through the ups and downs of their parent's addiction.

Do Surrender to God - Surrender and trust God with your loved one. Even if your situation does not change, you will be able to rest in the presence of God. At Teen Challenge we believe that God is the only One that can bring lasting change to a person's life. Letting go and trusting God with your loved one can be scary, but recognizing that He alone can change them will bring you peace and rest.

Don't Give up Hope - The stories of changed lives in this book are reminders that there is still hope no matter how long your loved one has been addicted. When you have a loved one struggling day after day, year after year it can seem as if change is impossible. It is important not to lose hope and faith during this time and to remember that God is able to do the impossible. There are times when an alcoholic or addict has been addicted for so many years that the family gives up all possibility of hope but nothing is impossible with God! Don't give up hope!

If you are reading this chapter and do not know Christ, I encourage you to read the salvation page at the end of the book. A life changing encounter and relationship with Jesus Christ is our greatest hope and is what will help you through your loved ones addiction.

Don't Stop Praying - The story below is from a mom who never stopped praying for her daughter. I trust these words from the heart of a mother will bring encouragement to your heart as you continue to pray for your loved ones. The Bible tells us to "always pray and not give up." (Luke 18:1)

Never Cease Praying

Where can I begin to tell you the story of how I almost lost my daughter completely to the world of sinful behavior and drugs? My name is Tabitha Louise Tripp, and let me tell you where it began. With prayer, lots of prayer!

When Jessie was in her last year of high school, she started doing her "own thing"; hanging with kids I didn't really approve of and smoking pot. As time went on, she began to alienate herself from us, moving from one relationship to another. We would see her occasionally, but never long enough to know how addicted she had really become. As always I kept her in my prayers but at this point I needed to have faith that God had her in his hands. After many years, she hit her "rock bottom." My daughter was living at home when, with the help of my pastor; I confronted her about her drug use. I didn't want to do anything to make her leave, so that night I prayed and asked God to help me be a parent and not a friend. It was then that I decided the tough love had to come into play. The next day I gave her an ultimatum, "If you are going to live here, then with my pastor's help, we need to get you into a detox and into a program." At first she resisted, not wanting anyone to know, but I stuck to my guns and kept saying if she wanted to live here this is what had to happen. It wasn't easy to do because I was afraid of losing her again, but I trusted God to have control of the whole situation.

My pastor and I both wanted to see her go to Teen Challenge, which is a 15 month program. She of course said no, that it was too long of a time. I once again had to lay down the law, but this time I said, "Give me three months in Teen Challenge and you can come home to live." She wasn't happy, but she agreed. During those three months I was always on my knees praying that God would get a hold of her heart and make her want to stay. There were days that I didn't want to get out of bed and but I prayed for strength and continued faith in God and His plan.

> The three months were up and I was ready to hear Jess ask to come home. But through the grace of God, she decided to stay and complete the program.

All I could keep saying through my happy tears was, "Thank you Jesus!"

Exercising tough love was the hardest thing I've had to do, but I knew if I enabled her and her addiction in any way, I would have lost her instead of helped her. Sometimes as a parent, we need to be the one to make decisions that our children are unable to make for themselves. Jess now understands that enrolling in Teen Challenge is what helped save her life.

So, never cease praying, even when you can't see the light at the end, have faith and never give up! I had hope, I had faith, and I had God to carry her through this. I had PRAYERS! May God Bless and give you all strength and courage in your situation.

Don't Blame Yourself - Families often blame themselves for their loved ones addiction. It is easy to live in a place of regret, contemplating all of the "could haves" and "should haves" throughout life. Every parent could have been a better parent, and every spouse could have been a better spouse, children could have been better children, but these aren't excuses to be addicted to drugs and alcohol. It would be wonderful if there was an eraser that could fix the past and all of its problems, but since that is not possible, we must make amends for the past and move forward to the future.

If you feel you have contributed to their addiction in some way, ask for their forgiveness. Today can be the day you move forward, ask forgiveness from your loved one and work on receiving God's grace and forgiveness for those things you regret. A person cannot move forward while still living in the past. You are not to blame for your loved one's addiction.

Don't Take the "Easy Road" - When your loved one is ready for help, they usually want to take the easy road or the path of least resistance, i.e. a short term program or program with limited rules and structure. Many addicts try other programs before coming to Teen Challenge. Teen Challenge is not a program for those who "need help," it is a program for those who "want help." It is a "challenging" program for those who are serious about wanting to change their lives. No lasting change comes easily. When your loved one is ready for help, encourage them not to take the easy path. Contact the Teen Challenge center nearest you to find help or referrals for your loved one.

Make a Difference!

1. Raise Your Level of Awareness:

Get training to help with prevention and intervention in the lives of those struggling!

2. Outreach In Your Local Community:

Bring hope by joining an experienced group doing outreach in your community, and reach out to those struggling with addiction, alcoholism and life controlling problems.

3. Become a Volunteer:

Contact the Teen Challenge Center nearest you for volunteer opportunities!

4. The Hope Line: 1-855-404-HOPE

Share the Teen Challenge HOPE line with someone you know that is struggling with addiction.

5. Prayer:

Pray for people to be set free from addiction and alcoholism, pray for the students, their families, and staff in our Teen Challenge homes.

An Investment in Lives that Pays Eternal Dividends

As a Shining Star, you can be a lifeline of encouragement and support to an addicted young person who is discovering God's love and a new life at Teen Challenge.

For just $1 a day/$30 a month, you can help underwrite the cost of a student in the residential, recovery program and give a man or woman in our homes real hope for a promising future without drugs or alcohol addiction!

Your partnership will be a tremendous encouragement to them as they are changed by a loving God from the inside out and become loving, healthy members of their families and a credit to their communities as caring, responsible and productive citizens without dependence on drugs or alcohol.

Call **508-408-4372**
to see how you can become a Student Sponsor!

Or visit our website: **www.tcnewengland.org**
to pledge your support.

Thank you!

TEEN CHALLENGE

CHANGING LIVES,
ONE CUP AT A TIME

For more information on purchasing our coffee, please contact:

Teen Challenge New England & New Jersey
1315 Main Street, Brockton, MA 02301
(508) 408-4378
info@tcnewengland.org
www.tcnewengland.org

*He gave his life to purchase freedom for everyone.
This is the message God gave to the world at just the right time.*
1 Timothy 2:6

END ADDICTION

JOIN THE FIGHT AGAINST DRUG AND ALCOHOL ABUSE

Overdoses are on the rise,
addiction has become an epidemic.
Too many promising lives have been lost.

The **End Addiction** campaign will raise awareness of this growing epidemic, help prevent young people from going down the path of addiction and offer **HOPE** to those trapped in addiction.

Addiction knows no bounds.
It affects people of all ages and from all walks of life.
If you or someone you know is struggling,
don't give up - change is possible!

Call the HOPE LINE today,

...so that every addict will know that there is **HOPE**.

CHANGED LIVES

Ten True Stories: ***From Addiction to Freedom***

Single Copy $15

Case of 32 $350 - Free Shipping

eBook Download $10

Buy both books for $25

Single Copy $15

Case of 32 $350 - Free Shipping

eBook Download $10

Get yours today at: **www.tcnewengland.org**

Book 3 Coming in 2016

NEED HELP?

If you or someone you know is struggling with drug addiction, alcoholism or a life controlling problem, Teen Challenge is here to help.

Call the Teen Challenge HOPE Line at

1-855-404-HOPE

to speak to someone today and to get hope and help!

TEEN CHALLENGE *Vehicle Donation*

HELP CHANGE A LIFE!
DONATE A VEHICLE TO TEEN CHALLENGE!

You can help save a life by donating your vehicle to Teen Challenge.
Every car, truck, mini-van, boat, etc.
we receive helps fund the life-changing program of Teen Challenge!

Donating your vehicle to Teen Challenge is simple.
Visit our website or call today!

Book Teen Challenge

Bring Teen Challenge to Your:

Church

Choir presentations including testimonies, singing, program information, and product sales.

School

Making Good Decisions and drug prevention presentation for students.

Community Drug Awareness Events

Table with drug information, students and/or staff to answer questions.

Contact the Teen Challenge Center nearest you today!

TEEN CHALLENGE - LOCATIONS

CORPORATE HEADQUARTERS
1315 Main Street
Brockton, MA 02301
P: 508-408-4378
F: 508-580-4186
info@tcnewengland.org
www.tcnewengland.org

Brockton, MA Men's Campus
1315 Main Street
Brockton, MA 02301
P: 508-586-1494
F: 508-580-4186
director@tcbrockton.org
www.tcbrockton.org

Boston, MA Men's Campus
16 Bloomfield Street
Dorchester, MA 02124
P: 617-318-1380
F: 617-318-1385
director@tcboston.org
www.tcboston.org

Maine Men's Campus
11 Hudson Lane
Winthrop, ME 04364
P: 207-377-2801
F: 207-377-2806
director@tcmaine.org
www.tcmaine.org

New Hampshire Men's Campus
147 Laurel Street
Manchester, NH 03103
P: 603-647-7770
F: 603-647-7570
director@tcnewhampshire.org
www.tcnewhampshire.org

Rhode Island Women's Campus
572 Elmwood Avenue
Providence, RI 02907
P: 401-467-2970
F: 401-461-3510
director@tcrhodeisland.org
www.tcrhodeisland.org

Connecticut Men's Campus
86 Spring Street
New Haven, CT 06534
P: 203-789-6172
F: 203-789-1127
director@tcconnecticut.org
www.tcconnecticut.org

Vermont Men's Campus
1296 Collins Hill Road
Johnson, VT 05656
P: 802-635-7807
F: 802-635-7029
director@tcvermont.org
www.tcvermont.org

New Jersey Men's Campus
245 Stanton Mountain Road
Lebanon, NJ 08833
P: 973-374-2206
F: 973-374-5866
director@tcnewjersey.org
www.tcnewjersey.org

Do you have freedom?

Those struggling with drug and alcohol addiction are not free and desperately need the help of Jesus to save them, free them and restore them! If you don't know Jesus, you too, need the freedom from sin and the weight of the world.

Why do I need to know Jesus?

God created us to be in relationship with Him. Adam and Eve enjoyed a beautiful closeness with their Creator, but something tragic happened. They chose to disobey and rebel against God. This caused separation between God and man. All have sinned and fall short of the glory of God (Romans 3:23).

What does this mean for me?

God loves us so much that He sent His son, Jesus, to live a sinless life on earth, and then to die as a sacrifice for the sin that we deserve punishment for. Now our hearts can be made new and we can be reconciled back into a right relationship with God. This is VERY good news! Will you accept this free gift of salvation from your Father who loves you unrelentingly?
(Romans 6:23) (John 3:16)

Where do I go from here?

To heaven when your life is over! Until then, walk with God, turn from sin, read the bible, get involved in church, talk with God regularly and tell people about this great news in your life.

"For Christ also suffered once for sins, the righteous for the unrighteous, that He might bring us to God." - 1 Peter 3:18 [ESV]